# Natural
# Gas

## Other books in the Fueling the Future series:

# Natural Gas

Carrie Fredericks, *Book Editor*

Christine Nasso, *Publisher*
Elizabeth Des Chenes, *Managing Editor*

**GREENHAVEN PRESS**
*An imprint of Thomson Gale, a part of The Thomson Corporation*

Detroit • New York • San Francisco • New Haven, Conn. • Waterville, Maine • London

**LIBRARY OF CONGRESS CATALOGING-IN-PUBLICATION DATA**

Natural gas / Carrie Fredericks, book editor.
  p. cm. --  (Fueling the future)
Includes bibliographical references and index.
ISBN-13: 978-0-7377-3598-7 (hardcover : alk. paper)
ISBN-10: 0-7377-3598-8 (hardcover : alk. paper)
1. Natural gas.   2. Gas as fuel.   I. Fredericks, Carrie.
TP350.N35 2006
553.2'85--dc22

                                                2006018867

Printed in the United States of America

# SOC
# Contents

## Chapter 1: The History and Development of Natural Gas

## Chapter 2: Does Natural Gas Use Harm the Environment?

## Chapter 3: Can Natural Gas Meet Future Energy Needs?

# Foreword

The wind farm at Altamont Pass in Northern California epitomizes many people's idea of wind power: Hundreds of towering white turbines generate electricity to power homes, factories, and businesses. The spinning turbine blades call up visions of a brighter future in which clean, renewable energy sources replace dwindling and polluting fossil fuels. The blades also kill over a thousand birds of prey each year. Every energy source, it seems, has its price.

The bird deaths at Altamont Pass make clear an unfortunate fact about all energy sources, including renewables: They have downsides. People want clean, abundant energy to power their modern lifestyles, but few want to pay the costs associated with energy production and use. Oil, coal, and natural gas contain high amounts of energy, but using them produces pollution. Commercial solar energy facilities require hundreds of acres of land and thus must be located in rural areas. Expensive and ugly transmission lines must then be run from the solar plants to the cities that need power. Producing hydrogen for fuel involves the use of dirty fossil fuels, tapping geothermal energy depletes groundwater, and growing biomass for fuel ties up land that could be used to grow food. Hydroelectric power has become increasingly unpopular because dams flood vital habitats and kill wildlife and plants. Perhaps most controversial, nuclear power plants produce highly dangerous radioactive waste. People's reluctance to pay these environmental costs can be seen in the results of a 2006 Center for Economic and Civic Opinion poll. When asked how much they would support a power plant in their neighborhood, 66 percent of respondents said they would oppose it.

Many scientists warn that fossil fuel use creates emissions that threaten human health and cause global warming. Moreover, numerous scientists claim that fossil fuels are running out. As a result of these concerns, many nations have begun to revisit the energy sources that first powered human enterprises.

In his 2006 State of the Union speech, U.S. President George W. Bush announced that since 2001 the United States has spent "$10 billion to develop cleaner, cheaper, and more reliable alternative energy sources," such as biomass and wind power. Despite Bush's positive rhetoric, many critics contend that the renewable energy sources he refers to are still as inefficient as they ever were and cannot possibly power modern economies. As Jerry Taylor and Peter Van Doren of the Cato Institute note, "The market share for non-hydro renewable energy . . . has languished between 1 and 3 percent for decades." Controversies such as this have been a constant throughout the history of humanity's search for the perfect energy source.

Greenhaven Press's Fueling the Future series explores this history. Each volume in the series traces the development of one energy source, and investigates the controversies surrounding its environmental impact and its potential to power humanity's future. The anthologies provide a variety of selections written by scientists, environmental activists, industry leaders, and government experts. Volumes also contain useful research tools, including an introductory essay providing important context, and an annotated table of contents that enables students to locate selections of interest easily. In addition, each volume includes an index, chronology, bibliography, glossary, and a Facts About section, which lists useful information about each energy source. Other features include numerous charts, graphs, and cartoons, which offer additional avenues for learning important information about the topic.

Fueling the Future volumes provide students with important resources for learning about the energy sources upon which human societies depend. Although it is easy to take energy for granted in developed nations, this series emphasizes how energy sources are also problematic. The U.S. Energy Information Administration calls energy "essential to life." Whether scientists will be able to develop the energy sources necessary to sustain modern life is the vital question explored in Greenhaven Press's Fueling the Future series.

# Introduction

The American West has long been a symbol of the nation's past, the frontier to which adventurers who dreamed of a better life could come to try their luck. Today, that frontier has become the center of intense debate as the nation struggles to meet growing energy needs. Large natural gas deposits have been found in Wyoming, Colorado, Montana, New Mexico, and Utah. However, these states also are home to some of the nation's most cherished national parks that are valued for their pristine open spaces. The natural gas industry argues that in order to keep pace with a rising demand for energy, the nation must open up these wild lands to gas drilling. They also maintain that more drilling is needed to reduce America's dependence on foreign sources of energy, a reliance that makes the country vulnerable to supply disruptions. Environmentalists disagree. They contend that such areas should be preserved for future generations. Environmentalists also claim that natural gas drilling and use harm the environment. Moreover, these critics assert, more drilling for finite fossil fuels such as natural gas only postpones the day when Americans will have to transition to renewable energy sources.

## The Finite Nature of Natural Gas

Natural gas is a fossil fuel. The gas was made millions of years ago from the bodies of dead plants and animals. As the organisms died, layers of sediment eventually covered them. Pressure from these layers, combined with heat from beneath the earth, transformed this organic material into coal, petroleum, and natural gas. These fossil fuel deposits are vast, but people have been extracting more of them each year. When the resources are exhausted, there simply will be no more. Despite the finite nature of fossil fuels, the world's developed countries depend almost entirely upon their use. Fossil fuels currently account for more than 80 percent of the world's fuel sources. Natural gas is used for almost 25 percent of fuel needs worldwide and accounts for more than 25 percent of daily fuel consumption in the United States. Central to the debate over natural gas drilling in the West is this finite nature of fossil fuels. While America's oil consumption has been growing, its domestic petroleum production has decreased, forcing the nation to import more of its oil from foreign countries. This increased dependency on oil-rich nations has energy experts and policy makers worried. They remember too well how energy dependency threatened the nation in the 1970s.

During that era, crude oil use declined as a result of the 1973 OPEC (Organization of Petroleum Producing and Exporting Countries) oil embargo, which severely limited the amount of available oil. As a result of contracting supplies, oil prices soared, sending shock waves throughout the economy. Energy

*Natural gas deposits have been found in some of the nation's most cherished parks, such as Moab, Utah, raising the question of whether to extract an energy resource or preserve natural beauty.*

experts and policy makers reacted by increasing investment in domestic natural gas drilling. Very quickly natural gas became the fuel of choice for industrial and home heating use. In the early 1980s new lands were opened up for gas drilling, and gas became cheaper as supplies became more plentiful. Today's push to open the West to gas drilling is also an attempt to reduce the country's dependence on foreign sources of oil.

Another development in the 1970s helped shape today's opposition to natural gas development in the West. The era saw the emergence of America's environmental movement. People became more aware of how modern life was harming the envi-

*A worker extracts natural gas from below the earth's surface. Natural gas has become an increasingly affordable and plentiful energy resource.*

# DRIVING UNDER THE AFFLUENCE

"Driving Under the Affluence," cartoon by Dan Wasserman. Copyright (c) April 2002 by the Boston Globe. Reproduced by permission of Knight Ridder/Tribune Information.

ronment, and they pushed to get environmental laws passed that would regulate industries, especially the energy industry. For example, environmentalists succeeded in getting passed stricter regulations on the quantity of emissions that power plants were allowed to produce. As a result, air pollution decreased significantly. Americans are still concerned that fossil fuel production and use is irreparably harming the environment. They are especially concerned about gas drilling in sensitive areas such as the West.

## The Gas Industry's Argument

The natural gas industry has attempted to address Americans' concerns by developing new technologies that make drilling less damaging. Industry leaders say that with these new technologies, natural gas can be extracted from even the most environmentally sensitive areas without adverse impacts. New drilling techniques, including smaller drilling bores and seismic imaging to help pinpoint natural gas beds, have made drilling less damaging to the environment, they say. Another positive development is directional drilling, which allows technicians to reach natural gas beds under water bodies without erecting derricks in the water body itself. Directional drilling minimizes water pollution, harm to aquatic life, and disruption of the fishing industry. The industry has also begun to use less harmful methods of keeping track of their wells. Wells can now be monitored with remote solar technology, which cuts down on the amount of vehicle traffic to and from the well. In addition, with smaller drilling heads becoming more popular, the amount of ground that a specific well occupies has become smaller. Some gas companies are also testing a new natural gas drilling rig that could reduce harmful emissions. According to Kim McGuire of the *Denver Post*, a gas company in Colorado "has been able to reduce flaring—the burning of excess gas—reducing pollutants by about 90 percent." Such technologies, the gas industry contends, make natural gas drilling in the American West more attractive. Capturing gas from beneath fragile lands can be accomplished, they say, with minimal impact.

## The Environmentalists' Argument

Environmental organizations have not accepted these arguments. They claim that the steps taken by drilling operators to minimize environmental impacts are not enough. These critics assert that any natural gas drilling, even that using the latest technology, requires a network of roads linking the drilling site with production and transportation facilities. These roads and the increased traffic that results from them damage the land, they maintain. Environmentalists also note that the noise of drilling operations can be heard for miles around a drilling site, disrupting wildlife. Drilling also produces large amounts of drilling sludge, mud that has been contaminated with chemicals used to lubricate the drilling borehole. Another drilling problem is the water used. In some types of drilling, vast amounts of water are pumped into the borehole to fracture a seam in the drilled rock to release the trapped gas. This water becomes contaminated and in turn contaminates underground water tables and other nearby water sources, environmentalists say.

While all of these concerns lead environmentalists to oppose drilling in the American West, perhaps the source of greatest

*A team drills for natural gas in a canyon. Environmentalists argue that such drilling operations irreparably harm the environment.*

consternation is air pollution. As *Los Angeles Times* reporter Miguel Bustillo writes in regard to Mount Rushmore in South Dakota, "It may soon be harder to see the famous faces through the man-made haze generated by the addition of 50,000 gas wells in northeastern Wyoming and southeastern Montana." Air pollution in the nation's natural parks, especially those located in the West, has become a growing concern. In an article in the *Denver Post*, McGuire reports, "From Wyoming to Colorado to New Mexico, state and federal officials say air pollution may be the first wide-scale environmental impact of the West's energy boom."

## The Duel Over the West

The battle between the gas industry and environmentalists over the West is growing more intense as the nation's energy needs continue to rise. Deciding whose arguments make the most sense can be difficult because both sides make valid points. In old Westerns, identifying the hero and the villain is easy. The bad guy acts solely for personal gain, and he does not care whom he hurts in his pursuit of self-interest. By contrast, the good guy stands up for the community, fighting for those who are being victimized. When the two men face each other in a duel, it is easy to know whom to root for.

In the new duel being fought in the West, determining which is the good guy and which is the bad is not as easy. The gas industry is responding to the nation's real need for more energy. Without more energy the economy could collapse, and Americans' way of life, which depends entirely on the easy availability of fossil fuels, could change for the worse. On the other hand, the industry's main concern—as is the case with all businesses—is to increase company profits. In the pursuit of such profits, energy companies do not always act in the public's best interest. On the other side of the debate are environmentalists. They are fighting to protect the wilderness that Americans value so highly, acting to make sure these pristine lands are left for the enjoyment of future generations. On the other hand, their actions lead to ever-greater restrictions on energy development, which can lead to supply shortfalls and rising prices.

The battle for the West will not be over any time soon. Deciding whether to drill for natural gas in America's most pristine lands will only become more difficult as the nation's economy—and hence its demand for energy—continues to grow. Perhaps the opposing sides in this saga will reach a compromise, one in which the nation obtains more of the vital energy it needs while still protecting the lands so cherished by the American people.

A worker balances on the suspension cables high above the Texas Illinois Natural Gas Company's pipeline suspension bridge.

CHAPTER 1

# The History and Development of Natural Gas

# How Natural Gas Is Formed and Extracted

## Neil Schlager and Jayne Weisblatt

In the following article, Neil Schlager and Jayne Weisblatt provide an overview of what natural gas is, how it was formed, and how it can be extracted and used. As extraction techniques improve, natural gas is becoming an increasingly versatile and vital energy source, write the editors. Once extracted, natural gas, according to Schlager and Weisblatt, can also be broken down into such component gases as methane and butane. Worldwide, more than 120 million metric tons of liquid natural gas are handled every year through production, importing, and shipping. Liquid natural gas is expected to have an annual growth rate of at least 10 percent during the next decade. Neil Schlager and Jayne Weisblatt are freelance editors.

## Natural Gas

Along with coal and petroleum, natural gas is one of the three main fossil fuels in use in the early twenty-first century. People use natural gas for heating, electrical power, and other purposes. Natural gas produces much less pollution than petroleum, so some people believe it could be an ideal substitute for petroleum and coal in the future.

Natural gas is a gaseous hydrocarbon. It is colorless, odorless, and lighter than air. Natural gas is made up of 75 percent methane, 15 percent ethane, and small amounts of other hydrocarbons such as propane and butane.

Neil Schlager and Jayne Weisblatt, eds., "Fossil Fuels," from *Alternative Energy*, vol. 1, Detroit: Thomson Gale, pp. 38–46.

The substance that oil companies sell as natural gas is almost pure methane, with the other gaseous components removed. When it burns, methane releases a large amount of energy, which makes it a useful fuel. Methane is sometimes called marsh gas because it forms in swamps as plants and animals decay underwater. Methane is naturally odorless, but gas companies add traces of smelly compounds to natural gas so that people will be able to smell gas leaks and avoid danger.

## Origins of Natural Gas

Natural gas formed from underwater plants and bacteria. These microscopic organisms fell to the bottom of the ocean when they died and over the course of millions of years were crushed and heated by the pressure of layers of sand, dirt, and other organic matter that accumulated on top of them. The mineral components of the undersea mud gradually turned into shale, and some of the organic components turned into natural gas. Natural gas can move around within porous reservoir rocks. It can also be trapped in underground reservoirs, or geologic traps. Natural gas is lighter than petroleum, so it usually sits on top of the petroleum in a reservoir. Natural gas sometimes seeps up through Earth's crust and appears on the surface.

## Finding and Extracting Natural Gas

Natural gas is usually found with petroleum. When geologists (scientists who deal with the history of Earth and its life as recorded in rocks) search for underground oil, they find natural gas along with it. Sometimes there are pockets of natural gas in coal beds. Geologists occasionally find reservoirs that contain mostly or all natural gas with no oil. The largest reserves of natural gas in the United States are in Texas, Alaska, Oklahoma, Ohio, and Pennsylvania. Some experts believe that there is enough natural gas in the Earth to last two hundred years, although much of this gas may be difficult to reach.

When they first began drilling for oil, people believed natural gas was an unpleasant by-product. They would burn the natural gas away before removing the oil from the ground. Now oil companies know that natural gas is a valuable commodity in its own right, and they extract it carefully. The process of drilling for

# How Natural Gas Is Formed

The sun is the ultimate source of energy.

Sea plants and animals die and sink to the ocean floor where they are buried in layers of sand and silt.

**OCEAN**
200-400 Million Years Ago

**OCEAN**
50-100 Million Years Ago

Over millions of years the remains become buried deeper, covered with more layers of sand and silt.

Heat and enormous pressure from these layers compress the remains and convert the long-stored sun's energy into gas.

natural gas is similar to that of drilling for petroleum. In many cases natural gas comes out of wells that have already been dug to extract oil. Oil companies also drill wells to extract natural gas by itself. There are three main kinds of natural gas wells:

- Gas wells, which are dug into a reservoir of relatively pure natural gas
- Oil wells, which are dug for extracting oil but also extract any natural gas that happens to be in the reservoir
- Condensate wells, which are dug into reservoirs that contain natural gas and a liquid hydrocarbon mixture called condensate but contain no crude oil

Natural gas that comes from oil wells is sometimes called associated gas. Natural gas from gas wells and condensate wells is called non-associated gas because it is extracted on its own and not as a by-product of oil drilling.

## Making Natural Gas Useful

The natural gas that consumers use is almost pure methane. The natural gas that comes out of a well is not pure and may contain a mixture of hydrocarbons and gases, including methane, ethane, propane, and butane. It also may contain small amounts of oxygen, argon, and carbon dioxide, but methane is by far the largest component.

An oil or gas company processing natural gas separates the gases into individual components, dividing them into pure methane, pure propane, pure butane, and so on. The liquid forms of the non-methane gas components, such as propane and butane, are called natural gas liquids, or NGLs, and sometimes are called liquid petroleum gas, or LPG. All of these products can be sold individually, so it is cost-effective to separate them.

The first step in processing is to remove any oil mixed with the gas. Natural gas that comes out of an oil well is separated from petroleum at the well. Sometimes the gas is dissolved in the oil, like the carbonation in a soft drink, and through the force of gravity the gas bubbles come out of the oil. In other cases the oil workers use a separator that applies heat and pressure to the mixed oil and gas to make them separate. The workers must also remove any water from the natural gas, using heat, pressure, or chemicals. They then remove NGLs using similar techniques.

Once they have been removed from natural gas, NGLs must be separated from one another. This is done through a process called fractionation, which involves boiling the NGLs until each one has evaporated. A similar process is used to refine petroleum. The different NGLs have different boiling points. As the NGLs boil, the different hydrocarbons evaporate and can be captured.

Some natural gas comes out of the ground with large amounts of sulfur in it. It is called sour gas because the sulfur makes the gas smell like rotten eggs. The gas company must remove the sulfur before selling the gas because sulfur in significant amounts is poisonous for humans to breathe and because it corrodes metal. The companies can sell the sulfur for industrial uses once it is separated out.

Sometimes a processing plant turns natural gas into liquid before transporting it. Liquid natural gas is one six-hundredth the volume of natural gas in gas form. Liquefying it makes it possible to store and transport natural gas around the world.

Once it has been refined and liquefied, natural gas can be transported and sold. The most common way to transport natural gas is through pipelines, which crisscross the United States and many other countries. If the gas is not sold right away, the gas company must store it. Natural gas is usually stored underground in formations such as empty gas reservoirs; in aquifers, or underground rock formations that hold water; and in salt caverns.

## Current and Potential Uses of Natural Gas

People have known about natural gas for thousands of years. The eternal flames in ancient temples may have been fueled by natural gas. In the early nineteenth century people began using natural gas as a light source, but as soon as oil was discovered in the 1860s and electricity became widespread, people abandoned natural gas except for limited use in cooking and heating.

Even so, the natural gas industry built the first large natural gas pipeline in 1891 and a large network of pipelines in the 1920s. Gas companies built more pipelines between 1945 and

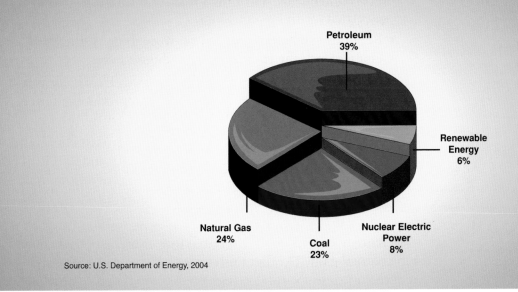

**U.S. Energy Consumption by Source**

Petroleum
39%

Renewable
Energy
6%

Natural Gas
24%

Coal
23%

Nuclear Electric
Power
8%

Source: U.S. Department of Energy, 2004

1970, which made it convenient to use natural gas for heating homes and for use in appliances.

Natural gas has become more appealing as a fuel in recent years. Some uses are:

- Powering heaters and air conditioners. Because so many homes and businesses use gas heat, natural gas consumption typically is much higher in the winter than in the summer.
- Running appliances such as water heaters, stoves, washers and dryers, fireplaces, and outdoor lights.
- Serving as an ingredient in plastics, fertilizer, antifreeze, and fabric.
- Producing methanol, butane, ethane, and propane, which can be used in industry and as fuel.
- Dehumidifying, or drying the air in, factories that make products that can be damaged by moisture.

Scientists are considering the use of natural gas in applications such as the following:

- Powering natural gas-fueled vehicles, which produce far fewer emissions than vehicles powered by gasoline.

- Powering fuel cells in which hydrogen is used to produce electricity with few emissions.
- Reburning, or adding natural gas to coal- or oil-fired boilers to reduce the emission of greenhouse gases.
- Cogeneration, a technology for generating electricity as it burns fuel, requiring less total fuel and producing fewer emissions.
- Combined cycle generation, a technology that captures the heat generated in producing electricity and uses it to create more electricity. Combined cycle generation units powered by natural gas are much more efficient than those powered by petroleum or coal.

Scientists are especially interested in technologies that combine natural gas with other fossil fuels to increase efficiency and reduce emissions. Natural gas is seen as a good source of fuel for the future, and as a result scientists are constantly inventing new ways to use it.

## Benefits of Natural Gas

Natural gas has advantages over petroleum and coal. It burns cleanly, producing no by-products except for carbon dioxide and water, so it does not cause the same degree of air pollution as the other fossil fuels. It does not produce the sludge that results from coal-burning emissions.

Natural gas can take the place of gasoline as a fuel for cars, trucks, and buses. Most natural gas vehicles are powered by compressed natural gas (CNG); the technology used to pump CNG into a car is almost identical to the process of fueling a gasoline-powered car. Some vehicles can use either gasoline or CNG. Natural gas cars have no trouble meeting environmental standards because of their low emissions. Natural gas is very safe; it does not pollute groundwater.

For many years natural gas has been cheaper than gasoline. Many cities have converted their buses, taxis, construction vehicles, garbage trucks, and public works vehicles to natural gas. These organizations are well suited to use natural gas as fuel because their vehicles do not travel long distances and can afford the cost of converting the vehicles in the first place.

## Drawbacks of Natural Gas

Natural gas historically was hard to transport and store, but modern technology has for the most part removed that difficulty. One reason natural gas is not a perfect substitute for petroleum is that supplies are limited. At current rates of use, all of the world's natural gas could be used up in forty to ninety years.

*Workers lay pipe that will deliver natural gas to homes, electric power plants, and other sites that require energy.*

Natural gas vehicles have not become widespread because it is more expensive to convert gasoline vehicles for natural gas use; there are very few natural gas refueling stations; and the vehicles cannot travel long distances without refueling.

## Impact of Natural Gas

Natural gas is the cleanest fossil fuel. The burning of natural gas releases no ash and produces low levels of carbon dioxide, carbon monoxide, and other hydrocarbons and very small amounts of sulfur dioxide and nitrogen oxides. Vehicles powered by natural gas emit 90 percent less carbon monoxide and 25 percent less carbon dioxide than gasoline-powered vehicles.

Natural gas is becoming an increasingly common fuel for electrical power plants and in industry. Electrical power plants fueled by natural gas produce far fewer emissions than coal-powered plants. Burning natural gas does not contribute significantly to the formation of smog.

Natural gas does contribute to some environmental problems. Burning natural gas emits carbon dioxide, which is considered a greenhouse gas that contributes to global warming. On the other hand, natural gas produces 30 percent less carbon dioxide than burning petroleum and 45 percent less carbon dioxide than burning coal, so it is still preferable to either of those.

On an economic level, the cost of natural gas has dropped considerably. The development of LNG technology means that natural gas is easier and less expensive to store and to transport, and liquefaction techniques (turning gas into a liquid) improve every year. Petroleum engineers are constantly getting better at finding and extracting natural gas from the ground.

Natural gas may change the way people use power in their daily lives. In the twenty-first century natural gas is a fairly minor fuel compared with gasoline, but it has the potential to be much more important. If power plants switch to the use of natural gas during summer when demand for natural gas is lowest and smog is highest, they could emit fewer pollutants and improve air quality. Using natural gas instead of other fossil fuels could reduce acid rain and particulate emissions. As people become concerned about emissions and fuel economy, they may want vehicles powered by natural gas. The vehicles will

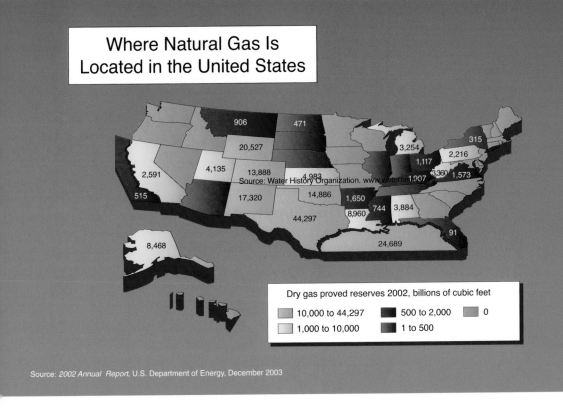

## Where Natural Gas Is Located in the United States

Source: Water History Organization. www.waterhistory.org

Dry gas proved reserves 2002, billions of cubic feet

| | |
| --- | --- |
| 10,000 to 44,297 | 500 to 2,000 |
| 1,000 to 10,000 | 1 to 500 |
| 0 | |

Source: *2002 Annual Report*, U.S. Department of Energy, December 2003

then become more widely available, less expensive, and easier to refuel.

## Issues, Challenges, and Obstacles in the Use of Natural Gas

Natural gas technology is not widespread. The fuel has many possible applications, but car manufacturers will have to decide that it is cost-effective for them to build natural gas vehicles before they do so on a large scale. Consumers will not buy natural gas vehicles until they are convinced that it will be convenient, safe, and inexpensive for them to buy natural gas as fuel. A final large issue is the supply of natural gas, which could run out in a few decades.

# The History of Natural Gas Use

## Natural Gas Supply Association

According to the Natural Gas Supply Association (NGSA) in the following selection, natural gas was known to ancient people across the world. The ancient Greeks saw lightning ignite natural gas, creating an ever-burning flame. More than twenty-five hundred years ago the Chinese used natural gas to heat water for desalination. The association explains that manufactured natural gas—gas made from coal—became available in the United States in the early 1800s. The first natural gas wells were dug in Fredonia, New York, in the 1820s. Mostly burned as a source of light, natural gas became easier to use with the invention of the Bunsen burner in 1885. This invention opened up opportunities for gas to be used for cooking and heating. Gas pipeline construction began in the 1890s, but it was not until reliable pipelines were built after World War II that natural gas was brought to most homes, the NGSA says. The Natural Gas Supply Association is an association of natural gas producers and marketers.

Natural gas is nothing new. In fact, most of the natural gas that is brought out from under the ground is millions and millions of years old. However, it was not until recently that methods for obtaining this gas, bringing it to the surface, and putting it to use were developed.

Before there was an understanding of what natural gas was, it posed somewhat of a mystery to man. Sometimes, such things

Natural Gas Supply Association, "History of Natural Gas," www.naturalgas.org, 2004. Reproduced by permission.

as lightning strikes would ignite natural gas that was escaping from under the earth's crust. This would create a fire coming from the earth, burning the natural gas as it seeped out from underground. These fires puzzled most early civilizations, and were the root of much myth and superstition. One of the most famous of these types of flames was found in ancient Greece, on Mount Parnassus approximately 1,000 B.C. A goat herdsman came across what looked like a 'burning spring', a flame rising from a fissure in the rock. The Greeks, believing it to be of divine origin, built a temple on the flame. This temple housed a priestess who was known as the Oracle of Delphi, giving out prophecies she claimed were inspired by the flame.

These types of springs became prominent in the religions of India, Greece, and Persia. Unable to explain where these fires

*The ancient Greeks built the Oracle of Delphi over a natural gas spring, believing it to be of divine origin.*

*A replica of Colonel Edwin Drake's well. Drake was the first person in North America to dig a well to harness the power of natural gas.*

came from, they were often regarded as divine, or supernatural. It wasn't until about 500 B.C. that the Chinese discovered the potential to use these fires to their advantage. Finding places where gas was seeping to the surface, the Chinese formed crude pipelines out of bamboo shoots to transport the gas, where it was used to boil sea water, separating the salt and making it drinkable.

## Natural Gas Goes Commercial

Britain was the first country to commercialize the use of natural gas. Around 1785, natural gas produced from coal was used to light houses, as well as streetlights.

Manufactured natural gas of this type (as opposed to naturally occurring gas) was first brought to the United States in 1816, when it was used to light the streets of Baltimore, Maryland. However, this manufactured gas was much less efficient, and less environmentally friendly, than modern natural gas that comes from underground.

Naturally occurring natural gas was discovered and identified in America as early as 1626, when French explorers discovered natives igniting gases that were seeping into and around Lake Erie. The American natural gas industry got its beginnings in this area. In 1859, Colonel Edwin Drake (a former railroad conductor who adopted the title 'Colonel' to impress the townspeople) dug the first well. Drake hit oil and natural gas at 69 feet below the surface of the earth.

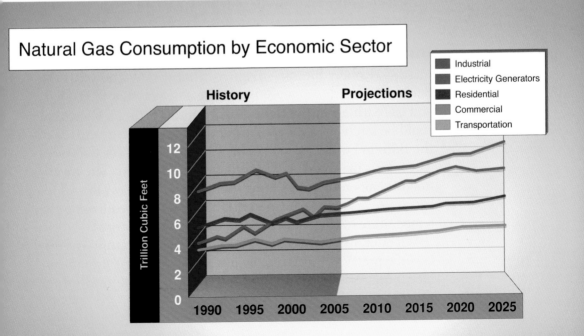

**Natural Gas Consumption by Economic Sector**

Legend:
- Industrial
- Electricity Generators
- Residential
- Commercial
- Transportation

History — Projections

Trillion Cubic Feet: 0, 2, 4, 6, 8, 10, 12

1990 1995 2000 2005 2010 2015 2020 2025

Source: *Annual Energy Outlook 2004*, U.S. Department of Energy, January 2004

Most in the industry characterise this well as the beginning of the natural gas industry in America. A two-inch diameter pipeline was built, running 5 and 1/2 miles from the well to the village of Titusville, Pennsylvania. The construction of this pipeline proved that natural gas could be brought safely and relatively easily from its underground source to be used for practical purposes.

In 1821, the first well specifically intended to obtain natural gas was dug in Fredonia, New York, by William Hart. After noticing gas bubbles rising to the surface of a creek, Hart dug a 27 foot well to try and obtain a larger flow of gas to the surface. Hart is regarded by many as the 'father of natural gas' in America. Expanding on Hart's work, the Fredonia Gas Light Company was eventually formed, becoming the first American natural gas company.

During most of the 19th century, natural gas was used almost exclusively as a source of light. Without a pipeline infrastructure, it was difficult to transport the gas very far, or into homes to be used for heating or cooking. Most of the natural gas produced in this era was manufactured from coal, as opposed to transported from a well. Near the end of the 19th century, with the rise of electricity, natural gas lights were converted to electric lights. This led producers of natural gas to look for new uses for their product.

## Bunsen's Burner

In 1885, Robert Bunsen invented what is now known as the Bunsen burner. He managed to create a device that mixed natural gas with air in the right proportions, creating a flame that could be safely used for cooking and heating. The invention of the Bunsen burner opened up new opportunities for the use of natural gas in America, and throughout the world. The invention of temperature-regulating thermostatic devices allowed for better use of the heating potential of natural gas, allowing the temperature of the flame to be adjusted and monitored.

Without any way to transport it effectively, natural gas discovered pre-WWII was usually just allowed to vent into the atmosphere, or burnt, when found alongside coal and oil, or simply left in the ground when found alone.

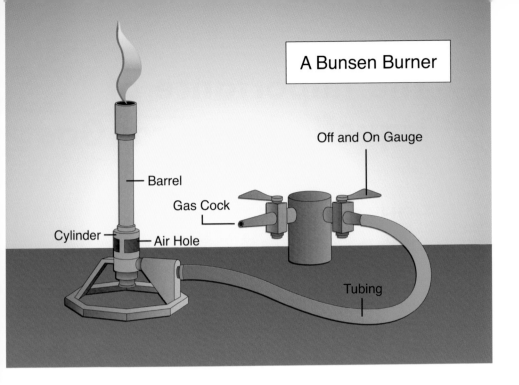

A Bunsen Burner

Barrel

Gas Cock

Off and On Gauge

Cylinder

Air Hole

Tubing

## Pipeline Construction Leads to Gas Transportation

One of the first lengthy pipelines was constructed in 1891. This pipeline was 120 miles long, and carried natural gas from wells in central Indiana to the city of Chicago. However, this early pipeline was very rudimentary, and was not very efficient at transporting natural gas. It wasn't until the 1920's that any significant effort was put into building a pipeline infrastructure. However, it wasn't until after World War II that welding techniques, pipe rolling, and metallurgical advances allowed for the construction of reliable pipelines. This post-war pipeline construction boom lasted well into the 60's, and allowed for the construction of thousands of miles of pipeline in America.

Once the transportation of natural gas was possible, new uses for natural gas were discovered. These included using natural gas to heat homes and operate appliances such as water heaters and oven ranges. Industry began to use natural gas in manufacturing and processing plants. Also, natural gas was used to heat boilers used to generate electricity. The transportation infrastructure had made natural gas easy to obtain, and it was becoming an increasingly popular form of energy.

# The Importance of Liquefied Natural Gas

### CH-IV International

CH-IV International explains in this selection that lique-fied natural gas (LNG) is a super-cooled version of traditional natural gas. When cooled to −260°F, natural gas condenses to liquid form. The liquid has a much smaller volume than traditional natural gas, which allows LNG to be transported in tankers from areas farther than can be reached by natural gas pipelines. A few accidents involving LNG explosions occurred in the 1970s, but with a greater understanding about how gases can be liquefied safely, no new accidents have occurred recently, CH-IV International explains. CH-IV International specializes in liquefied natural gas import and export.

When natural gas is cooled to a temperature of approximately −260°F at atmospheric pressure it condenses to a liquid called liquefied natural gas (LNG). One volume of this liquid takes up about 1/600th the volume of natural gas at a stove burner tip. LNG weighs less than one-half that of water, actually about 45% as much. LNG is odorless, colorless, non-corrosive, and non-toxic. When vaporized it burns only in concentrations of 5% to 15% when mixed with air. Neither LNG, nor its vapor, can explode in an unconfined environment.

## The Makeup of LNG

Natural gas is composed primarily of methane (typically, at least 90%), but may also contain ethane, propane and heavier hydrocarbons. Small quantities of nitrogen, oxygen, carbon dioxide, sulfur compounds, and water may also be found in "pipeline" natural gas. The liquefaction process removes the oxygen, carbon dioxide, sulfur compounds, and water. The process can also be designed to purify the LNG to almost 100% methane.

## How Is It Stored?

LNG tanks are always of double-wall construction with extremely efficient insulation between the walls. Large tanks are low aspect ratio (height to width) and cylindrical in design with a domed roof. Storage pressures in these tanks are very low, less than 5 psig (pounds per square inch gauge). Smaller quantities, 70,000 gallons and less, are stored in horizontal or vertical, vacuum-jacketed, pressure vessels. These tanks may be at pressures any where from less than 5 psig to over 250 psig. LNG must be maintained cold (at least below −117°F) to remain a liquid, independent of pressure.

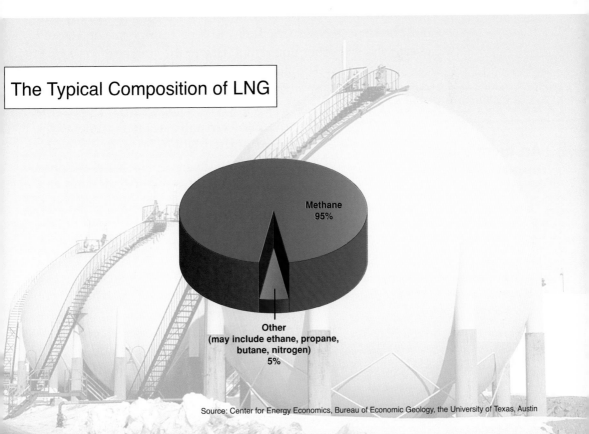

The Typical Composition of LNG

Methane
95%

Other
(may include ethane, propane,
butane, nitrogen)
5%

Source: Center for Energy Economics, Bureau of Economic Geology, the University of Texas, Austin

## How Is It Kept Cold?

The insulation, as efficient as it is, will not keep the temperature of LNG cold by itself. LNG is stored as a "boiling cryogen," that is, it is a very cold liquid at its boiling point for the pressure it is being stored. Stored LNG is analogous to boiling water, only 470° colder. The temperature of boiling water (212°F) does not change, even with increased heat, as it is cooled by evaporation (steam generation). In much the same way, LNG will stay at near constant temperature if kept at constant pressure. This phenomenon is called "autorefrigeration". As long as the steam (LNG vapor boil off) is allowed to leave the tea kettle (tank), the temperature will remain constant.

If the vapor is not drawn off, then the pressure and temperature inside the vessel will rise. However, even at 100 psig, the LNG temperature will still be only about −200°F.

## Have There Been Any Serious LNG Accidents?

First, one must remember that LNG is a form of energy and must be respected as such. Today LNG is transported and stored as safely as any other liquid fuel. Before the storage of cryogenic liquids was fully understood, however, there was a serious incident involving LNG in Cleveland, Ohio in 1944. This incident virtually stopped all development of the LNG industry for 20 years. The race to the Moon led to a much better understanding of cryogenics and cryogenic storage with the expanded use of liquid hydrogen (−423°F) and liquid oxygen (−296°F). LNG technology grew from the National Aeronautics and Space Association's advancement.

In addition to Cleveland, there have been two other U.S. incidents sometimes attributed to LNG. A construction accident on Staten Island in 1973 has been cited by some parties as an

*A liquefied natural gas (LNG) storage tank. LNG is a very cold liquid that is stored at its boiling point.*

"LNG accident" because the construction crew was working inside an (empty, warm) LNG tank. In another case, the failure of an electrical seal on an LNG pump in 1979 permitted gas (not LNG) to enter an enclosed building. A spark of indeterminate origin caused the building to explode. As a result of this incident, the electrical code has been revised for the design of electrical seals used with all flammable fluids under pressure.

## What Is CNG?

Compressed natural gas (CNG) is natural gas pressurized and stored in welding bottle-like tanks at pressures up to 3,600 psig (pounds per square inch gauge). Typically, it is the same composition of the local "pipeline" gas, with some of the water removed. CNG and LNG are both delivered to the engines as low pressure vapor (ounces to 300 psig). CNG is often misrepresented as the only form of natural gas that can be used as vehicle fuel. LNG can be used to make CNG. This process requires much less capital intensive equipment and about 15% of the operating and maintenance costs.

## What Is LPG?

Liquid petroleum gas (LPG, and sometimes called propane) is often confused with LNG and vice versa. They are not the same

*LNG tankers such as this one deliver liquefied natural gas to destinations all over the world.*

and the differences are significant. LPG is composed primarily of propane (upwards to 95%) and smaller quantities of butane. LPG can be stored as a liquid in tanks by applying pressure alone. LPG is the "bottled gas" often found under BBQ grills. LPG has been used as fuel in light duty vehicles for many years. Many petrol stations in Europe have LPG pumps as well.

# CHAPTER 2

# Does Natural Gas Use Harm the Environment?

The liquefied natural gas plant in Bontang, Borneo, Indonesia, was built on the edge of a mangrove swamp.

# Opening the Great Lakes to Gas Drilling Would Harm the Environment

## Public Interest Research Group in Michigan

In the following article the Public Interest Research Group in Michigan contends that reopening the Great Lakes to gas and oil drilling will harm the environment. Gas spills are routine occurrences, according to PIRGIM, and drilling wastes contain toxic chemicals that can contaminate the environment. Leaks and spills also pose a serious human health threat, the organization contends. Rather than drill for natural gas, PIRGIM argues, America should conserve energy and develop renewable and clean energy sources. The Public Interest Research Group in Michigan is a public interest group concentrating on issues involving the environment, government, and the economy.

With recent attempts to reopen the Great Lakes to oil and gas drilling, Michigan faces a significant new threat to its economy, environment, and health. Both offshore drilling—currently banned in Michigan—and directional drilling in the Great Lakes pose unacceptable risks and hazards. Drilling in Michigan's Great Lakes would have significant long-term and short-term negative impacts on the lake's watershed, regardless of the drilling method employed.

Public Interest Research Group in Michigan, "Dirty Drilling; The Threat of Oil and Gas Drilling in Michigan's Great Lakes, Executive Summary," *Public Interest Research Group in Michigan*, 2003, pp. 1–6.

## Environmental Impacts

Natural gas and oil leaks and spills can have extremely negative effects on the natural environment, both on and off shore.
Past safety records from drilling sites across the country indi-
cate that such accidents will take place—it is a matter of when
it will happen, not if it will happen. The potential for accidental or routine release of drilling wastes into the environment is
alarming. Releases can occur through containment failure, runoff, pipeline accidents, and direct discharge.

Routine drilling wastes, such as drilling muds, cuttings, and
produced waters, contain both profuse and varied toxic chemicals that pose significant risks to the environment. These risks

*An aerial view of the Great Lakes. Although the lakes
contain storages of natural gas, opening them to drilling
could cause irreparable damage.*

to wildlife include developmental defects, shortened lifespan, and physiological changes. Many of the toxic chemicals associated with oil and gas drilling can accumulate and magnify in the food chain. This poses a risk to aquatic organisms higher in the food chain, such as fish and birds. Furthermore, many of these chemicals tend to persist in the environment, leading to long-term, chronic exposure for aquatic organisms.

## Economic Impacts

An expansion of oil and gas drilling would likely have a net negative effect on the economy of the Great Lakes region. The annual value of all oil and gas drilling in Michigan—including the small portion that currently takes place under the Great Lakes—is $2 billion, compared to the $11.5 billion spent by tourists traveling 100 miles or more to Michigan locations in 1999.

Oil and gas drilling under the Great Lakes can adversely affect the lake economy in several ways. Oil and gas drilling could lower water quality, both through routine operations and accidental leaks and spills, and would lead to direct conflicts with nearby water-related recreational uses. These impacts could negatively affect the boating and recreational fishing industries, which pump a combined $2.5 billion in consumer spending into the state's economy annually—about a third of which is directly attributable to activities on the Great Lakes.

Moreover, Michigan's water resources are the most frequently cited positive impression created by the state with Midwestern tourists. Thus, real or perceived declines in Great Lakes water quality caused by drilling could reduce the state's appeal to outside visitors, whether or not they partake in water-related recreational activities.

Expanded oil and gas drilling under the Great Lakes would also not bring significant additional revenue to the state. State officials estimate that expanded drilling would bring a total of $100 million in additional revenue to the Michigan Natural

*Tourists recreate along Like Michigan. Some argue that drilling for natural gas under the Great Lakes would threaten Michigan's tourism industry.*

Resources Trust Fund, compared to annual state general fund-general purpose revenues of $9.1 billion.

## Human Health Impacts

While the human health impacts of leaks and spills are primarily local in nature, placement of wells onshore puts human health at greater risk from accidents, as well as from routine pollution and discharges. People can also be exposed to toxic chemicals from routine drilling wastes, such as drilling muds and cuttings. As pollutants from oil and gas drilling build up in the food chain, people who consume fish from the Great Lakes will be at serious risk of health problems such as genetic defects and cancer. Routine discharge or accidental release of these materials could be devastating in the densely populated areas of the Great Lakes watershed.

Northern Michigan residents have already experienced negative impacts from the release of poisonous hydrogen sulfide gas from onshore and directional natural gas wells. At least 24 people, five of them children, have been seriously injured due to hydrogen sulfide releases in northern Michigan.

Routine discharges and accidental spills of toxic chemicals from drilling sites can also contaminate the water of the Great Lakes, thus contaminating a primary drinking water source for millions of Michigan residents. Some of these discharges, such as air emissions and runoff, are an unavoidable consequence of oil and gas drilling. Discharge need not occur in the water to impact the water quality. In fact, discharges in the Great Lakes drainage basin can be as significant as discharges directly into the lake. . . .

## Canadian Drilling in the Great Lakes

The Canadian experience of drilling for natural gas and oil on the Canadian side of Lake Erie serves as a cautionary example for Michigan. Spills associated with the petroleum industry are both widespread and highly significant environmental threats

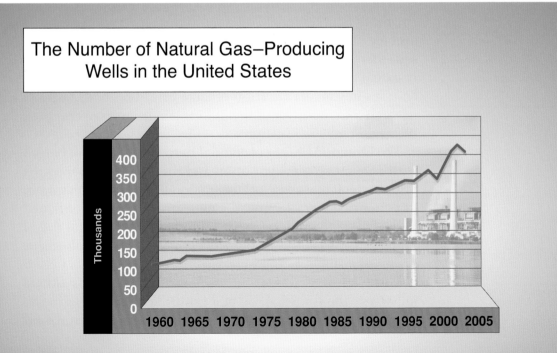

Source: *Annual Energy Review*, 2003, U.S. Department of Energy

to the Canadian Great Lakes. Fifty-one natural gas spills directly associated with gas drilling in Canada's portion of Lake Erie were documented between 1997 and 2001—an average of almost one spill a month. The volume of natural gas released and the full duration of the leaks were not reported to or by the Canadian government.

The Canadian side of Lake Erie was also impacted by 83 petroleum spills from all sectors between 1990 and 1995 (the last year for which data was made available for this report). The volume spilled was not known for at least one-third of the spills. In addition, only 45% of the contaminants were cleaned up, on average.

The routine, long-term discharge of drilling wastes from drilling in Canada's portion of Lake Erie represents a significant environmental hazard. These direct discharges into Lake Erie have subjected aquatic organisms to immediate and long-term health risks, ranging from localized fish kills to aquatic organism developmental impairment. These risks are exacerbated by the routine usage of toxic chemicals during oil and gas drilling.

## Canadian Reporting

Canadian regulations that track the usage and disposal of toxic chemicals (the National Pollutant Release Inventory) expressly exclude oil and gas drilling operations from reporting. As a result, there is no publicly available data regarding the quantity or extent of toxic chemical usage in the natural gas drilling operations in Canada's portion of Lake Erie. This both restricts research into the safety of the drilling and hampers oversight of that industry.

The Ontario Ministry of Natural Resources, which is charged with regulatory oversight of oil and gas drilling, has shown a historic trend towards a lack of environmental consideration in its permitting. For example, the ministry was severely criticized for its failure to implement the Ontario Environmental Bill of Rights, effectively thwarting citizen access to and involvement in environmental decision-making.

Finally, there is a significant lack of data about the systemic impacts of the Canadian oil and gas drilling operations in the Great Lakes. Neither Canadian nor American governmental

*A fish from Lake Erie. The habitats of fish and other marine creatures could be threatened by natural gas drilling in the Great Lakes.*

agencies have investigated the impacts of existing drilling operations over the past 20 years. Despite this lack of readily accessible data, information pieced together from the Canadian Coast Guard, the Ontario Ministry of Natural Resources, and the Ontario Ministry of Environment demonstrates severe impacts.

## Recommendations for the Future

Based on the findings of this report, oil and gas drilling in or under the Great Lakes would pose unacceptably high environmental, economic, and public health risks. Many of these risks are inherent to the oil and gas drilling process and, as such, cannot be mitigated by regulatory changes or management practices. As a result, PIRGIM [Public Interest Research Group in Michigan] Education Fund recommends that Michigan enact a permanent ban on directional drilling under the Great Lakes and maintain its ban on offshore drilling.

Rather than relying on dirty drilling to meet Michigan's energy demands, the state should invest in a cleaner, smarter energy future by promoting energy efficiency and renewable energy. This can be undertaken with the following: tax rebates and incentives for the purchase of energy efficiency appliances; updated energy efficiency requirements in Michigan's building codes; tax rebates and incentives for the installation of small-scale renewable energy generation equipment; and passage of a Renewable Portfolio Standard that requires 10% of the electricity sold in Michigan come from renewable sources by 2010 and 20% by 2020. By investing in energy efficiency and renewable energy, Michigan can permanently protect the Great Lakes, further protect our other environmental resources, and save Michigan residents money.

# Gas Drilling in the Great Lakes Need Not Harm the Environment

## Michael Barratt

> According to Michael Barratt in the following selection, gas drilling in the Great Lakes area can be conducted without harming the environment. Existing wells illustrate that drilling need not put the environment or human health in danger. Moreover, the gas companies currently drilling the Great Lakes pay royalties that are used to preserve environmentally sensitive areas, he points out. Barratt is a contributor to the Great Lakes Radio Consortium, an environmental radio outlet on Michigan Radio in Ann Arbor, Michigan.

People around the Great Lakes have seen quantum jumps in the price of energy within the last few months. . . . Natural gas prices have increased 40–60%, and propane prices have increased markedly.

Since Michigan only produces 4% of its crude oil demand and 30% of its natural gas demand, we need to find ways to both conserve and maintain our energy supply.

## Proposals to Help Meet Michigan's Energy Needs

The Michigan Department of Natural Resources (DNR) has proposed to lease land under the Great Lakes for the purpose of

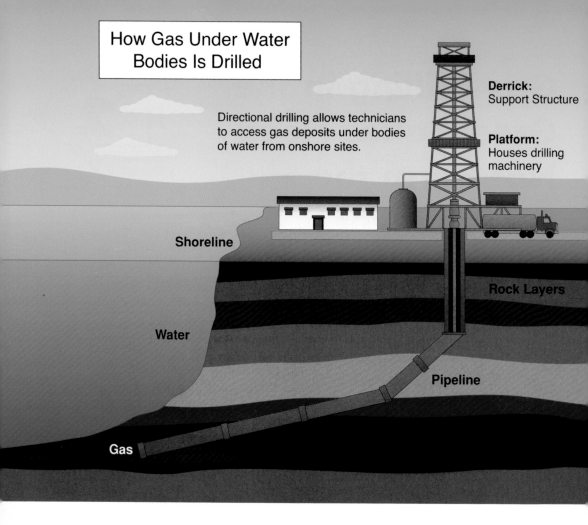

## How Gas Under Water Bodies Is Drilled

Directional drilling allows technicians to access gas deposits under bodies of water from onshore sites.

**Derrick:** Support Structure

**Platform:** Houses drilling machinery

Shoreline

Rock Layers

Water

Pipeline

Gas

drilling wells from onshore locations. The proposed procedures require new wells to be located at least 1,500 feet from the shoreline. They also require that sites be screened, and no drilling is to be permitted in dune areas, floodplains, or environmentally sensitive areas.

Additional wells drilled under Great Lakes waters may encounter significant reserves to help Michigan have a secure energy supply. Using a safe and proven technology known as directional drilling, it is possible to reach and produce these reserves with little to no effect on the surrounding areas. There have been 13 wells drilled under Great Lakes waters from onshore locations since 1979. Seven of those wells, which are still producing, have produced 439,000 barrels of oil and more than 17 billion cubic feet of gas. There have been no spills, accidents, or incidents associated with the wells since they have been drilled.

## Drilling Benefits

New wells drilled under Great Lakes waters, if drilling is allowed, could produce an additional 90 billion cubic feet of gas, and 2 million barrels of oil; enough to heat more than 1 million homes and fuel 157,500 cars for a year. We now have a window of opportunity to use existing infrastructure associated with the currently producing wells to develop some of the additional reserves under the Great Lakes. Drilling pads, roads,

*A hiker enjoys a trail in a Michigan park. Some experts believe drilling for natural gas would not mar the area's natural beauty.*

pipelines, and production facilities are in place that can be used to drill new wells under the Great Lakes.

Besides energy security, the people of Michigan benefit from royalties paid to the State of Michigan. That money is put into the Michigan Natural Resources Trust Fund to develop and extend parks, and to purchase wetlands and other environmentally sensitive areas. The seven wells currently producing have contributed more than $16,000,000 to the Fund. Additional wells drilled under the Great Lakes could contribute another $85,000,000–$100,000,000.

## Drilling for the Future

Let's develop the State's Bottomland resources now in a safe and environmentally friendly way to ensure that Great Lakes waters and shorelines can be enjoyed by future generations and also to make sure we have the energy supplies here to maintain our quality of life.

# Drilling for Natural Gas in the Arctic National Wildlife Refuge Will Harm the Environment

**3**

## The Wilderness Society

In the following selection the Wilderness Society argues that drilling for natural gas and oil would negatively impact the wildlife in the Arctic National Wildlife Refuge. Toxic spills and miles of roads and pipelines would destroy this pristine land, the society argues. Affected animals would include polar bears, caribou, oxen, and migratory birds. The Wilderness Society is an environmental organization focused on the preservation of wilderness areas.

There is no other place on earth quite like the rolling tundra, rugged Brooks Range, boreal forests, coastal lagoons and barrier islands of the 19.6 million-acre Arctic National Wildlife Refuge in northeastern Alaska. Within the refuge, the 1.5-million-acre coastal plain is often referred to as "America's Serengeti" and like its African counter-part, it sustains an immense herd of large migratory mammals. The 130,000-strong Porcupine caribou herd uses the coastal plain of the refuge as its annual calving grounds, traveling hundreds of miles from wintering grounds in Canada and the U.S. More than 200 animal

The Wilderness Society, "Energy and Public Lands Report: Arctic National Wildlife Refuge, Alaska," www.wilderness.org, April 11, 2006. Reproduced by permission.

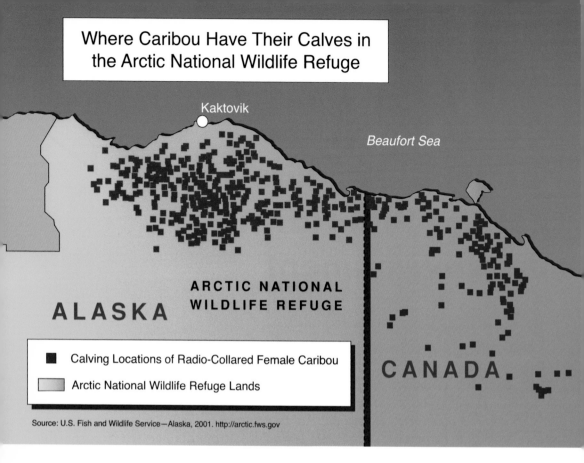

## Where Caribou Have Their Calves in the Arctic National Wildlife Refuge

Kaktovik

Beaufort Sea

ARCTIC NATIONAL
WILDLIFE REFUGE

ALASKA

CANADA

■ Calving Locations of Radio-Collared Female Caribou

▢ Arctic National Wildlife Refuge Lands

Source: U.S. Fish and Wildlife Service—Alaska, 2001. http://arctic.fws.gov

species, including polar and grizzly bears, wolves, muskoxen, and millions of migratory birds also dwell within the coastal plain.

Until now, the coastal plain of the refuge has remained virtually free of any human development enabling this very special land to continue to exist as it has for millennia, like almost no other region of the United States today. This nursery ground for caribou and other wildlife is sacred to the Gwich'in people—a nation of 7,000 Athabascan Indians who live in a village near the refuge. Caribou are at the center of the Gwich'in culture.

The U.S. Fish and Wildlife Service has called the refuge's Coastal Plain "the center for wildlife activity" for the entire refuge.

## The Birth of ANWR

In 1960, President Dwight D. Eisenhower created what was then called the Arctic National Wildlife Range to preserve the area's "unique wildlife, wilderness, and recreational values." Twenty years later, Congress expanded the refuge as part of the Alaska National Interest Lands Conservation Act. The act also directed studies of the refuge coastal plain's wilderness, wildlife, and its oil and gas reserves. It prohibited oil and gas development without a further act of Congress.

## Threats to the Refuge

Since the late 1980s, the oil industry and its allies in Congress have tried to pass legislation that would open the coastal plain of the Arctic Refuge to drilling. In 1995 Congress passed a massive budget bill that included a coastal plain drilling provision, but former President [Bill] Clinton vetoed it, citing his objection to the drilling scheme. Despite surveys that show a solid majority of Americans oppose drilling in the refuge, President [George W.] Bush has repeatedly stated his desire to open this

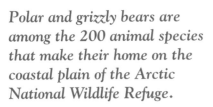

*Polar and grizzly bears are among the 200 animal species that make their home on the coastal plain of the Arctic National Wildlife Refuge.*

treasured land to development and he has made drilling there the centerpiece of his national energy strategy. . . .

## Gas Development Would Destroy the Refuge

According to a 1998 report from the U.S. Geological Survey, the mean estimate for the amount of oil that could be economically recovered from beneath the refuge at projected oil prices is 3.2 billion barrels—less than what the U.S. consumes in six months. At no time would oil from the refuge be expected to supply more than two percent of America's demand. None of this oil could reach consumers for at least 10 years.

*Swans float above the Arctic National Wildlife Refuge. Opening the refuge to drilling is one of the most contentious environmental issues in America today.*

The USGS' (U.S. Geological Survey's) mean estimate for technically recoverable natural gas from the refuge is 7 trillion cubic feet—about what the U.S. consumes in four months. None of this gas was projected to be economically recoverable. By comparison, the National Petroleum Council estimated a natural gas resource base in the lower-48 states of 1,466 trillion cubic feet. Even after subtracting gas estimated to occur in federal land areas that are protected from drilling, this is enough gas to meet America's estimated needs for 40 years.

**ANOTHER OPINION**

### No Solution to Energy Woes

"Opening a largely untouched refuge to industrial activity would destroy its unique wildlife and environment while contributing little to resolving the nation's energy woes."

Charles Pope, *Seattle Post-Intelligencer*, February 28, 2005.

The oil industry claims it can develop the Arctic Refuge in an "environmentally sensitive" manner and points to its history in Prudhoe Bay. But according to the Alaska Department of Environmental Conservation, oil companies emit more than a spill a day of oil and other toxic substances, and emissions of some air pollutants are twice as much as those found in Washington, D.C.

Oil or gas development in the Arctic Refuge would forever destroy this treasured land as wilderness with hundreds of miles of roads and pipelines, oil and other toxic spills, and the construction of infrastructure for thousands of workers.

# Drilling for Natural Gas in the Arctic National Wildlife Refuge Would Not Harm the Environment

**Paul K. Driessen**

According to Paul Driessen in the following article, it is time to drill for natural gas in the Arctic National Wildlife Refuge (ANWR) in Alaska. The plains of Alaska could hold vast amounts of recoverable gas and oil. With only two thousand acres being drilled out of 19 million acres, the ecological impact on the environment would be minimal, Driessen maintains. Rising energy costs make apparent the necessity for drilling in ANWR. Driessen is a senior policy adviser for the Congress of Racial Equality and Center for the Defense of Free Enterprise. He is also author of *Eco-Imperialism: Green Power, Black Death.*

The budget reconciliation bill recently passed by the US Senate [in 2005] would finally open the Arctic National Wildlife Refuge (ANWR) to drilling. Environmentalists are "outraged," while most Democrats in the House of Representa-

Paul K. Driessen, "It's Time to Support ANWR Drilling," www.enterstage right.com, December 19, 2005. Reproduced by permission of the author.

tives plan to go against their constituents' best interests by voting against drilling [they did].

Sadly, that's to be expected. What's amazing is that a number of House Republicans are likewise saying they intend to vote to lock up ANWR'S vast energy resources. They're supposed to understand market forces and energy economics—at least better than their colleagues across the aisle. And yet they are planning to cast "nay" votes precisely when global demand for petroleum is soaring, energy prices are reaching all-time highs, and winter heating bills will make it increasingly difficult for poor people to heat and eat.

That any responsible member of Congress could vote against this energy development legislation underscores the ideological blinders worn by drilling opponents, the vast misinformation that still dictates discussions about this issue, and the refusal of elected officials even to acknowledge the cumulative effects of "environmental protection" rules enacted over many decades— much less do anything about them.

## Those Who Oppose Drilling Are Hypocrites

Many votes against drilling will come from California, Northeastern and Midwestern legislators who have made a career of railing against high energy prices, "obscene" oil company profits, unemployment and balance of trade deficits—while simultaneously doing everything possible to constrict supplies, increase demand and drive up prices. For instance, air quality rules—coupled with a virtual prohibition on building new nuclear plants—mean that most new electrical generating plants are gas-fired. So demand for natural gas continues to climb, while domestic supplies continue to decrease.

But these same legislators have consistently opposed natural gas (and oil) development in Alaska, off the East Coast, off the Florida coast, along the Pacific Coast, in the Great Lakes, throughout the western states, and in any other areas where petroleum might actually be found.

They apparently believe it's OK to drill in other countries, even in sensitive areas in other countries. It's likewise appropriate to buy crude from oil-rich dictators (especially when offered

*It is argued that drilling for energy resources in other countries' lands (such as the Amazon, pictured) sends American jobs and money overseas.*

at a discount by Venezuelan despots), send American jobs and dollars overseas, reduce US royalty and tax revenues, imperil industries that depend on petroleum, and blanket habitats with "ecologically friendly" wind turbines and solar panels. However, drilling in the USA, even for natural gas, is strictly verboten.

This is truly political theater of the absurd.

## ANWR Has a Lot of Oil and Gas

ANWR, government geologists say, could hold up to 16 billion barrels of recoverable oil. That's 30 years' of imports from Saudi Arabia. Turned into gasoline, it would power California's entire vehicle fleet for some 50 years. The area's natural gas could fuel Florida, New Hampshire, New York, Pennsylvania and Wisconsin generating plants for a decade or more.

At $50 a barrel, ANWR crude would eliminate the need to import $800 billion worth of foreign oil, create up to 700,000 American jobs, and generate hundreds of billions in royalties and taxes.

Bringing this oil online would have another vital benefit. As Prudhoe Bay [Alaska] and nearby oil reserves decline, a point will be reached where there isn't enough to keep the Trans-Alaska Pipeline running at capacity. That would mean enormous quantities of otherwise recoverable oil will be left in the ground, instead of fueling our economy. New supplies from ANWR would ensure that our oil lifeline remains open.

*The Trans-Alaska pipeline, which stretches eight hundred miles, has been an important part of America's energy program, accounting for 25 percent of annual oil production.*

But all that is irrelevant, insist environmental purists in and out of Congress. Energy development would "irreparably destroy" the refuge, they assert. Caribou droppings.

## The Ecological Impact Would Be Minimal

ANWR covers 19 million acres, an area equivalent to South Carolina. Of this, only 2,000 acres—scattered in small parcels across the "coastal plain"—would actually be disturbed by drilling and development, thanks to modern directional drilling technologies. That's 0.01% of the refuge, one-twentieth of Washington, DC—or 20 of the buildings Boeing uses to manufacture 747 jets!

The potentially oil-rich area is flat, treeless tundra—3,500 miles from DC and 50 miles from the beautiful mountains seen in all the deliberately misleading anti-drilling photos. During eight months of winter, when drilling would take place, virtu-

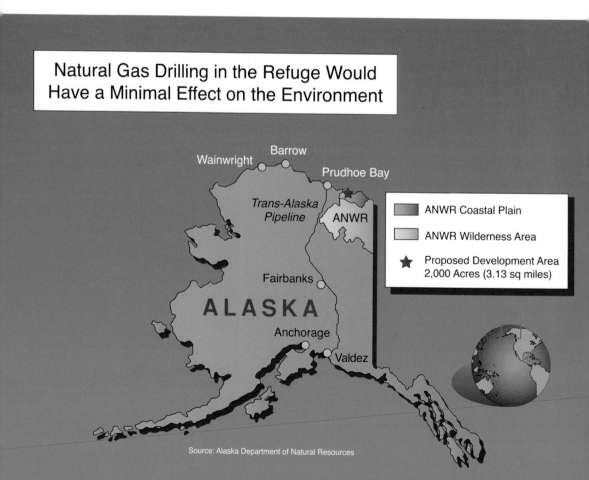

**Natural Gas Drilling in the Refuge Would Have a Minimal Effect on the Environment**

Barrow
Wainwright
Prudhoe Bay
Trans-Alaska Pipeline
ANWR
Fairbanks
ALASKA
Anchorage
Valdez

ANWR Coastal Plain
ANWR Wilderness Area
★ Proposed Development Area 2,000 Acres (3.13 sq miles)

Source: Alaska Department of Natural Resources

ally no wildlife are present. Only oil field workers are crazy enough to remain outdoors when temperatures drop to minus 40°F (Fahrenheit), the tundra turns rock solid, and that chaw of tobacco they spit out freezes before it hits the ground.

However, these unforgiving conditions mean drilling can be done with ice airstrips, roads and platforms. In the spring, they'll all melt, leaving only puddles and little holes. The caribou will return—just as they have for years at the nearby Prudhoe Bay and Alpine oil fields—and do just what they always have: eat, hang out and make babies. In fact, Prudhoe's caribou herd has increased from 6,000 head in 1978 to 32,000 today. Other Arctic wildlife will also return, along with the Alaska state bird, Mosquito giganteus (which locals claim can carry off rabbits and small dogs).

## The Bottom Line

Vast oil and gas potential, in a distant, mostly desolate area. Unprecedented global demand for petroleum. Soaring energy prices that hurt productivity, prosperity and the poor. Modern technological marvels that enable us to find and develop petroleum resources with no significant environmental impacts. Jobs, revenues and reduced dependence on foreign sources. Ensuring that we can recover all the oil we've already discovered along Alaska's North Slope.

The benefits are many and obvious. The negatives few. Finding and producing ANWR's oil ought to be a slam-dunk. The fact that so many congressmen (and senators) can't bring themselves to support drilling there—or anywhere else in or off our 50 states—ought to make every American question the analytical skills of the people they've sent to Washington.

Every thoughtful taxpayer and voter ought to tell their representatives: These oil and gas resources are vital to our future. It's time to end the obstruction and political posturing. It's time to drill in ANWR.

# CHAPTER 3

# Can Natural Gas Meet Future Energy Needs?

*A workman looks over the spinning section of pipe on a drilling platform in Silt Mesa, Colorado.*

# Natural Gas Can Supply America's Future Energy Needs

## Natural Gas Supply Association

The Natural Gas Supply Association argues in this viewpoint that advances in natural gas technology will ensure that the industry can meet the growing demand for energy. Progress in finding, extracting, processing, and transporting natural gas continues to make this energy source viable. Moreover, the association contends, new uses for natural gas, including to power hydrogen fuel cells, are expanding the potential of natural gas. The Natural Gas Supply Association is an association of natural gas producers and marketers.

Over the past thirty years, the oil and natural gas industry has transformed into one of the most technologically advanced industries in the United States. New innovations have reshaped the industry into a technology leader, in all segments of the industry. This [viewpoint] will discuss the role of technology in the evolution of the natural gas industry, focusing on technologies in the exploration and production sector, as well as a few select innovations that have had a profound effect on the potential for natural gas.

In recent years, demand for natural gas has grown substantially. However, as the natural gas industry in the United States becomes more mature, domestically available resources become harder to find and produce. As large, conventional natural gas deposits are extracted, the natural gas left in the ground is

Natural Gas Supply Association, "Natural Gas and Technology," www.natural gas.org, 2004. Reproduced by permission.

commonly found in less conventional deposits, which are harder to discover and produce than has historically been the case. However, the natural gas industry has been able to keep pace with demand, and produce greater amounts of natural gas despite the increasingly unconventional and elusive nature. The ability of the industry to increase production in this manner has been a direct result of technological innovations. Below is a brief list of some of the major technological advancements that have been made recently:

## Advances in the Exploration and Production Sector

Technological innovation in the exploration and production sector has equipped the industry with the equipment and practices necessary to continually increase the production of natural gas to meet rising demand. These technologies serve to make the exploration and production of natural gas more efficient, safe, and environmentally friendly. Despite the fact that natural gas deposits are continually being found deeper in the ground, in remote, inhospitable areas that provide a challenging environment in which to produce natural gas, the exploration and production industry has not only kept up its production pace, but in fact has improved the general nature of its operations. Some highlights of technological development in the exploration and production sector include:

- 22,000 fewer wells are needed on an annual basis to develop the same amount of oil and gas reserves as were developed in 1985.
- Had technology remained constant since 1985, it would take two wells to produce the same amount of oil and natural gas as one 1985 well. However, advances in technology mean that one well today can produce two times as much as a single 1985 well.
- Drilling wastes have decreased by as much as 148 million barrels due to increased well productivity and fewer wells.
- The drilling footprint of well pads has decreased by as much as 70 percent due to advanced drilling technology, which is extremely useful for drilling in sensitive areas.

*Oil rig workers manipulate heavy machinery to extract natural gas and oil from deep within the earth.*

- By using modular drilling rigs and slimhole drilling, the size and weight of drilling rigs can be reduced by up to 75 percent over traditional drilling rigs, reducing their surface impact.
- Had technology, and thus drilling footprints, remained at 1985 levels, today's drilling footprints would take up an additional 17,000 acres of land.
- New exploration techniques and vibrational sources mean less reliance on explosives, reducing the impact of exploration on the environment.

*Drill workers use the latest technology to extract natural gas from the earth. Technological innovation has helped make natural gas extraction more cost-effective and environmentally friendly.*

## Technological Innovations in Exploration and Production

- *3-D and 4-D Seismic Imaging*—The development of seismic imaging in three dimensions greatly changed the nature of natural gas exploration. This technology uses traditional seismic imaging techniques, combined with powerful computers and processors, to create a three-dimensional model of the subsurface layers. 4-D seismology expands on this, by adding time as a dimension, allowing exploration teams to observe how subsurface characteristics change over time. Exploration teams can now identify natural gas prospects more easily, place wells more effectively, reduce the number of dry holes drilled, reduce drilling costs, and cut exploration time. This leads to both economic and environmental benefits.

- *CO2-Sand Fracturing*—Fracturing techniques have been used since the 1970s to help increase the flow rate of natural gas and oil from underground formations. $CO_2$-Sand fracturing involves using a mixture of sand propants and liquid $CO_2$ to fracture formations, creating and enlarging cracks through which oil and natural gas may flow more freely. The $CO_2$ then vaporizes, leaving only sand in the formation, holding the newly enlarged cracks open. Because there are no other substances used in this type of fracturing, there are no 'leftovers' from the fracturing process that must be removed. This means that, while this type of fracturing effectively opens the formation and allows for increased recovery of oil and natural gas, it does not damage the deposit, generates no below ground wastes, and protects groundwater resources.

- *Coiled Tubing*—Coiled tubing technologies replace the traditional rigid, jointed drill pipe with a long, flexible coiled pipe string. This greatly reduces the cost of drilling, as well as providing a smaller drilling footprint, requiring less drilling mud, faster rig set up, and reducing the time normally needed to make drill pipe connections. Coiled tubing can also be used in combination with slimhole drilling to provide very economic drilling conditions, and less impact on the environment.

- *Measurement While Drilling*—Measurement-While-Drilling (MWD) systems allow for the collection of data from the bottom of a well as it is being drilled. This allows engineers and drilling teams access to up to the second information on the exact nature of the rock formations being encountered by the drill bit. This improves drilling efficiency and accuracy in the drilling process, allows better formation evaluation as the drill bit encounters the underground formation, and reduces the chance of formation damage and blowouts.

- *Slimhole Drilling*—Slimhole drilling is exactly as it sounds; drilling a slimmer hole in the ground to get to natural gas and oil deposits. In order to be considered slimhole drilling, at least 90 percent of a well must be drilled with a drill bit less than six inches in diameter (whereas conventional wells typically use drill bits as large as 12.25 inches in diameter). Slimhole drilling can significantly improve the efficiency of drilling operations, as well as decrease its environmental impact. In fact, shorter drilling times and smaller drilling crews can translate into a 50 percent reduction in drilling costs, while reducing the drilling footprint by as much as 75 percent. Because of its low cost profile and reduced environmental impact, slimhole drilling provides a method of economically drilling exploratory wells in new areas, drilling deeper wells in existing fields, and providing an efficient means for extracting more natural gas and oil from undepleted fields.

- *Offshore Drilling Technology*—The offshore oil and gas production sector is sometimes referred to as 'NASA of the Sea', due to the monumental achievements in deepwater drilling that have been facilitated by state of the art technology. Natural gas and oil deposits are being found at locations that are deeper and deeper underwater. Whereas offshore drilling operations used to be some of the most risky and dangerous undertakings, new technology, including improved offshore drilling rigs, dynamic positioning devices and sophisticated navigation systems are allowing safe, efficient offshore drilling in waters more than 10,000 feet deep. . . .

## Natural Gas Fuel Cells

Fuel cells powered by natural gas are an extremely exciting and promising new technology for the clean and efficient generation of electricity. Fuel cells have the ability to generate electricity using electrochemical reactions as opposed to combustion of fossil fuels to generate electricity. Essentially, a fuel cell works by passing streams of fuel (usually hydrogen) and oxidants over electrodes that are separated by an electrolyte. This produces a chemical reaction that generates electricity without requiring the combustion of fuel, or the addition of heat as is common in the traditional generation of electricity. When pure hydrogen is used as fuel, and pure oxygen is used as the oxidant, the reaction that takes place within a fuel cell pro-

*Advances in offshore drilling techniques have allowed the extraction of natural gas from more than ten thousand feet below the ocean's surface.*

duces only water, heat, and electricity. In practice, fuel cells result in very low emission of harmful pollutants, and the generation of high-quality, reliable electricity. The use of natural gas powered fuel cells has a number of benefits, including:

- *Clean Electricity*—Fuel cells provide the cleanest method of producing electricity from fossil fuels. While a pure hydrogen, pure oxygen fuel cell produces only water, electricity, and heat, fuel cells in practice emit only trace amounts of sulfur compounds, and very low levels of carbon dioxide. However, the carbon dioxide produced by fuel cell use is concentrated and can be readily recaptured, as opposed to being emitted into the atmosphere.

- *Distributed Generation*—Fuel cells can come in extremely compact sizes, allowing for their placement wherever electricity is needed. This includes residential, commercial, industrial, and even transportation settings.

- *Dependability*—Fuel cells are completely enclosed units, with no moving parts or complicated machinery. This translates into a dependable source of electricity, capable of operating for thousands of hours. In addition, they are very quiet and safe sources of electricity. Fuel cells also do not have electricity surges, meaning they can be used where a constant, dependable source of electricity is needed.

- *Efficiency*—Fuel cells convert the energy stored within fossil fuels into electricity much more efficiently than traditional generation of electricity using combustion. This means that less fuel is required to produce the same amount of electricity. The National Energy Technology Laboratory estimates that, used in combination with natural gas turbines, fuel cell generation facilities can be produced that will operate in the 1 to 20 Megawatt range at 70 percent efficiency, which is much higher than the efficiencies that can be reached by traditional generation methods within that output range.

The generation of electricity has traditionally been a very polluting, inefficient process. However, with new fuel cell technology, the future of electricity generation is expected to change dramatically in the next ten to twenty years. Research and development into fuel cell technology is ongoing, to ensure that the technology is refined to a level where it is cost effective for all varieties of electric generation requirements.

The natural gas industry is joined by government agencies and laboratories, private research and development firms, and environmental technology groups in coming up with new technologies that may improve the efficiency, cost-effectiveness, and environmental soundness of the natural gas industry.

# Natural Gas Cannot Supply America's Future Energy Needs

## Richard Heinberg

In the following excerpt from his book, *The Party's Over*, Richard Heinberg discusses whether natural gas can take the place of oil as a main energy source. Since both are finite fuels, is there enough to go around? As more drilling occurs and production drops off, some industry analysts suggest that United States Energy Information Agency estimates of a fifty-year supply of natural gas are much less favorable than originally thought. Several things may help to close the gap on the amount of natural gas available now, including a pipeline from Alaska and the increased use of LNG. But the public is consuming more and more gas each year and that means natural gas prices will increase to keep up with consumption. The term "transition fuel," instead of replacement, is used in this article and that may best describe the future way of looking at natural gas.

Richard Heinberg is a member of the Core Faculty of New College of California. He is the author of five books dealing with energy and science.

In some respects, natural gas appears to be an ideal replacement fuel for oil: it burns more cleanly (though it still produced $CO_2$); automobiles, trucks, and buses can be converted to run on it; and it is energy-dense and versatile. Its EROEI

Richard Heinberg, *The Party's Over: Oil, War and the Fate of Industrial Societies*, Gabriola Island, BC: New Society Publishers, 2003.

[Energy Return on Energy Invested] is quite high. It has long been used to create nitrogen fertilizers for agriculture (through the Haber-Bosch process), for industrial processes like glass-making, for electricity generation, and for household cooking and heating. Currently, natural gas accounts for about 25 percent of the US energy consumption; 17 percent of the gas extracted is used to generate electricity. Thus there already is an infrastructure in place to make use of this fuel.

Could extraction be increased to make up for the projected shortfalls in oil? Some organizations and individuals claim there is enough gas available globally to last for many decades. Estimates for total reserves vary from about 300 to 1,400 tcf (trillion cubic feet). With such a wide range of figures, it is clear that methods of reporting and estimating are imprecise and speculative. The number 1,100 tcf is often cited; this would represent 50 years' worth of reserves at current rates of global usage. The ever-optimistic Energy Information Agency (EIA) reports that the US also had about 50 years' worth of natural gas, with proven reserves of 177.4 tcf in 2001. As of 2001, annual usage was in the range of 23 tcf.

Clearly, the EIA is assuming considerable future discovery, as current proven reserves would last fewer than ten years of current usage rates. That assumption—that future discoveries will more than quadruple current proven reserves—is highly questionable.

## Are Outlooks Favorable?

Many industry analysts believe the outlook for future discoveries in North America is far less favorable than EIA forecasts suggest. In the decade from 1977 to 1987, 9,000 new gas fields were discovered, but the following decade yielded only 2,500 new fields. This general downward trend in discovery is continuing, despite strenuous efforts on the part of the industry. Matthew Simmons has reported that the number of drilling rigs in the Gulf of Mexico grew by 40 percent between April 1996 and April 2000, yet production remained virtually flat. That is largely because the newer fields tend to be smaller; moreover, because of the application of new technology, they tend to be depleted faster than was the case only a decade or two ago;

As natural gas drilling and production increase, some industry analysts worry that the supply will become exhausted.

new wells average a 56 percent depletion rate in the first year of production.

In a story dated August 7, 2001, Associated Press business writer Brad Foss noted that in the previous year, "there were 16,000 new gas wells drilled, up nearly 60 percent from 10,400 drilled in 1999. But output only rose about 2 percent over the same period, according to estimates from the Energy Department. The industry is on pace to add 24,000 wells by the end of the year, with only a marginal uptick expected in production."

In June 1999, *Oil and Gas Journal* described how the Texas gas industry, which produces one-third of the nation's gas, had to drill 6,400 new wells that year to keep production from plummeting. Just the previous year, only 4,000 wells had to be drilled to keep production steady.

According to Randy Udall of the Community Office for Resource Efficiency in Aspen, Colorado, "[n]o one likes talking about [natural-gas] depletion; it is the crazy aunt in the attic, the emperor without clothes, the wolf at the door. But the truth is that drillers in Texas are chained to a treadmill, and they must run faster and faster each year to keep up."

## Gas from Canada Goes South

US natural gas production has been in decline for years; in order to make up the shortfall, the nation has had to increase its imports from Canada, and Canada is itself having to drill an increasing number of wells each year just to keep production steady—a sign of a downward trend in discovery. A May 31, 2002 article by Jeffrey Jones for Reuters, entitled "Canada Faces Struggle Pumping More Natgas to US," begins ominously: "Canadian natural gas production may have reached a plateau just as the country's role as supplier to the United States is becoming more crucial due to declining US gas output and rising demand. . . ."

Furthermore, Mexico has already cut its gas exports to the US to zero, and has become a net importer of fuel.

A gas pipeline from Alaska could help, but not much. A three-foot-diameter pipeline moving gas at 2,200 feet per second would deliver only 0.5 tcf per year, less than two percent of the projected needs for the year 2020.

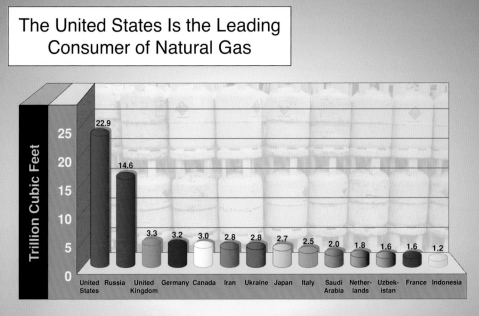

**The United States Is the Leading Consumer of Natural Gas**

Trillion Cubic Feet

| | |
|---|---|
| United States | 22.9 |
| Russia | 14.6 |
| United Kingdom | 3.3 |
| Germany | 3.2 |
| Canada | 3.0 |
| Iran | 2.8 |
| Ukraine | 2.8 |
| Japan | 2.7 |
| Italy | 2.5 |
| Saudi Arabia | 2.0 |
| Netherlands | 1.8 |
| Uzbekistan | 1.6 |
| France | 1.6 |
| Indonesia | 1.2 |

Source: *Annual Energy Review*, 2003, U.S. Department of Energy

## LNG as an Option

Ninety-nine percent of the natural gas used in the US is extracted in North America. While gas is more abundant in the Middle East, which has over a third of the world's reserves, gas is not easily transported by ship. It must be cooled to minus 260 degrees Fahrenheit (minus 176 degrees Celsius) during the journey, requiring special liquid-natural gas (LNG) tankers and ports. There are currently only three such ports in the US.

Moreover, nearly all of the existing LNG shipping capacity is spoken for by Japan, Korea, and Taiwan through long-term contracts. Europe and the Far East may be able to depend on gas from the Middle East for several decades to come, but that is probably not a realistic prospect for the US.

## Public Awareness Begins

The public got its first hint of a natural gas supply problem in the latter months of 2000, when the wellhead price shot up by 400 percent. This was a more dramatic energy price increase than

*A barge delivers liquid natural gas (LNG) to energy consumers. The demand for LNG could be outpacing its available supply.*

even the oil spikes of the 1970s. Homeowners, businesses, and industry all suffered. This gas crisis, together with simultaneous oil price hikes, helped throw the nation—and the world—into recession. Farmland Industries shut down some of its fertilizer plants because it could not afford to use expensive natural gas to make cheap fertilizer; many consumers were dismayed to find that their utility bills had doubled. A frenzy of new drilling resulted, which, together with a scaling back of demand due to the recession, enabled the natural gas market to recover so that prices eased back. Yet by the spring of 2001, wellhead gas prices were still twice what they had been twelve months earlier, and gas in storage had reached its lowest level ever.

The increasing demand for gas is coming largely from an increasing demand for electricity. To meet growing electricity needs, utilities in 2000–2001 ordered 180,000 megawatts of gas-fired power plants to be installed by 2005. This strategy seemed perfectly logical to the utilities' managers since burning gas is currently the cheapest and cleanest way to convert fossil fuel into electricity. But apparently no one in the industry had bothered to inquire whether there will be enough gas available to fire all of those new generators over their useful lifetime. Many exploration geologists are doubtful. By mid-2002, plans for many of those new gas-fired plants were being cancelled or delayed. . . .

## Is Natural Gas the Problem Solver?

Natural gas will not solve the energy-supply problem caused by oil depletion; rather, it may actually compound that problem. Our society is already highly dependent on natural gas and becoming more so each year. There are disturbing signs that rates of natural gas extraction in North America will soon start on an inexorable downhill slope—perhaps within a few months or at most a few years. When that happens, we may see a fairly rapid crash in production rather than the slow ramp-down anticipated for oil.

Many alternative energy advocates have described natural gas as a "transition fuel" whose increased usage can enable the nation to buy time for a switch to renewable energy sources. However, in view of the precarious status of North American gas supplies, it seems more likely that any attempt to shift to natural gas as an intermediate fuel would simply waste time and capital in the enlargement of an infrastructure that will soon be obsolete anyway—while also quickly burning up a natural resource of potential value to future generations.

# Increased Drilling Is Necessary to Meet Future Energy Needs

## John Riordan

In the following selection John Riordan argues that America has plenty of recoverable natural gas still available. However, those resources are not being adequately exploited, he contends. He believes that the nation needs more pipelines to move gas from where it is drilled to where it is needed. He also urges the government to invest in new technologies that will enable the recovery of harder-to-recover natural gas. Finally, Riordan maintains that the gas industry needs access to public lands where natural gas exists. Riordan is retired president and CEO of the Gas Technology Institute, an organization offering research, development, and training to the natural gas industry. He wrote this article for the Federation of American Scientists, which promotes the humanitarian use of science and technology.

When the Chairman of the Federal Reserve testified before Congress, we got a realistic assessment of the natural gas dilemma this country faces. Last June's [2003] message from Chairman Greenspan on Capitol Hill was loud and clear: the nation has to increase its supplies of natural gas or face the economic consequences.

John Riordan, "Meeting Natural Gas Demand: Infrastructure Is Important, Technology Is Key," FAS *Public Interest Report,* vol. 56, Autumn 2003, pp. 1–4. All rights reserved 2005—Federation of American Scientists. Reproduced by permission.

Let me first point out that, warnings aside, the US is not running out of natural gas. In fact, we have abundant gas reserves. At today's consumption rates, our 1400 trillion cubic feet of technically recoverable reserves would translate into almost 60 years of supply. The problem: We have essentially "cherry-picked" the inexpensive gas and need new ways to affordably meet gas demand.

## The Keys to More Natural Gas

There are three key ingredients to increasing gas supply. First, we need an expanded infrastructure, specifically to move Alaska's gas to the lower 48 via pipeline, as well as to enable increased imports of liquefied natural gas. Second, we need to re-visit federal policies and Congressional moratoria that have placed much of our potential gas supply off limits to production. Finally—and too often undervalued—we need to promote the research that will help us develop our abundant domestic natural gas reserves.

## Technology Critical to New Drilling Techniques

Technology was not, however, undervalued by Chairman Greenspan. It was, in fact, a key subtext of his testimony. He noted the value of technology to gas supply in observing that "dramatic changes in technology are making existing energy reserves stretch further while keeping long-term energy costs lower than they otherwise would have been." New techniques allow far deeper drilling of promising fields, especially offshore. He went on to highlight some of those technologies, along with their specific natural gas supply impacts. He noted that in the Rocky Mountain region, "technologies are facilitating production of tight sands and coalbed methane. Marketed production in Wyoming, for example, has risen from 3.4 percent of total US output, in 1996 to 7.1 percent last year."

> **ANOTHER OPINION**
>
> ### Future Energy Needs Require More Drilling
>
> "To secure adequate future energy supplies the U.S. must encourage more energy exploration and drilling. [Drilling in the Arctic National Wildlife Refuge] is just a start. There is over a 50 years supply of natural gas in the Outer Continental Shelf, which will require more drilling off Florida and the Gulf Coast."
>
> David Hogberg and James Dellinger, *American Spectator*, December 8, 2005.

*Workers drill for natural gas. It is argued that increased drilling is necessary to meet America's growing energy demands.*

## Research and Development Is Crucial

The development of technologies to produce gas from unconventional resources—tight gas sands, coalbed methane gas shales—was not serendipitous. Rather, it was a result of government and industry collaboration: a focused research effort, combined with critical production incentives, to enable the affordable production of resources that now represent over 20% of our domestic gas supply.

Unfortunately, trends in both government and industry are working against this need. Government funding for gas supply R&D (research and development) has not exceeded $15 million a year for a decade. Also, federal funding for oil and gas supply research is often viewed as corporate welfare. The problem with this view is that there is nothing in deregulated energy markets that either incentivizes or compels private R&D investment, in spite of the significant public policy ramifications associated with supply shortages and price spikes.

On the industry side, one of the unintended victims of deregulation of the production sector of the natural gas industry has been R&D. Company research budgets, found almost exclusively in the super-majors or in large service companies, have been declining for the last ten years. Also, major integrated oil and gas producers have largely moved offshore or overseas. This

*New drilling techniques make it possible to find natural gas fields deep under the ocean, which could help satisfy the growing demand for energy.*

*This stretch of public land in Colorado holds natural gas reserves, but there is controversy over whether to extract the gas and how to go about doing it.*

has left onshore production increasingly in the hands of small independent producers who lack the resources to conduct R&D.

Finally, collaborative industry research and development funding, paid for through a pipeline surcharge for the last 25 years, is slated for extinction in 2005. This fee funded a significant portion of the research that has enabled us to turn coalbed methane from a safety hazard into over 7% of our domestic production, or tight gas sands from a known but inaccessible resource, into 17% of our supply.

## Research Needed to Drill Unconventional Gas Basins

Significant—but expensive—gas reserves are found on federal lands in ultra-deepwater provinces offshore and in unconventional basins onshore. Congress should consider investing a portion of the federal oil and gas royalty monies currently going into the general fund into the research programs necessary to affordably produce these vast reserves. Analysis conducted by the Bureau of Economic Geology at the University of Texas, indicates that such an investment would result in substantial new gas supply, as well as a significant overall increase in revenues to the Treasury in the form of royalties on new, technology-enabled production.

## Answering the Wake-Up Call

Chairman Greenspan is correct in noting that, in addition to technology, we need additional infrastructure. We need responsible access to public lands currently open for production. But the political will may not be there to exploit these options. Infrastructure additions always encounter local resistance. Opening up offshore California, Florida or East Coast may—or may not—ever materialize. Also, the imports of natural gas in the form of LNG [liquefied natural gas] raise serious geopolitical issues, similar to those we currently have with oil.

Investing in developing the technologies we need to affordably produce our domestic gas resources in environmentally sound ways is critical, it is possible, and has been proven effective time and time again. We should heed Chairman Greenspan's entreaty on the need for gas supply and invest in the technologies we need to respond to this wake-up call.

# Increased Drilling Cannot Solve America's Energy Crisis

### Natural Resources Defense Council

According to the Natural Resources Defense Council in the following selection, the United States should not increase gas drilling. Rather, wasting less gas is the best way to reduce America's dependence on this fossil fuel. America should also ensure that natural gas production remains safe. Drilling in environmentally sensitive areas is not necessary since most areas containing gas are already open to drilling and exploration. Moreover, pipelines must be constructed to eliminate leaks and they should not be routed through sensitive habitats. The Natural Resources Defense Council is a national environmental and public health action organization.

Natural gas is used in a variety of ways, including as a source for heating, as fuel for electricity generation, and even as a power source for buses and other motor vehicles. It is the cleanest burning fossil fuel, particularly when modern equipment is used. But as with other fossil fuels, extracting and burning natural gas causes various forms of pollution. Natural gas is

Natural Resources Defense Council, "Creating a Responsible Natural Gas Policy," Natural Resources Defense Council, April 2005, pp. 17–20. Copyright © 2005 Natural Resources Defense Council. Reproduced by permission.

not sufficiently clean to be considered the long-term answer to America's energy needs, but it can act as a bridge to greater reliance on cleaner and renewable forms of energy.

Growing demand and sharp increases in short-term natural gas prices in 2004 have prompted some to call for more drilling on public lands and fewer environmental safeguards on gas exploration and use. Yet sacrificing our natural heritage and circumventing public participation in energy plans on public lands are simply not necessary in order to power our economy and homes.

The best way to reduce our economy's vulnerability to high natural gas prices is to waste less gas. . . . Simply by issuing new efficiency standards for commercial air conditioners, residential furnaces and boilers, and electric distribution transformers, America would save 6.4 trillion cubic feet of natural gas over the next 20 years.

Even with efficiency measures in place, however, America will continue to need natural gas. To ensure that natural gas is obtained in the safest and most sustainable way, America must take the following steps:

## Do Not Drill in Sensitive Offshore Areas

According to the most recent Department of Interior assessment, 80 percent of economically recoverable gas reserves in offshore areas are now open to development. Only a portion of America's most important national coastal treasures—from Big Sur to the Florida Keys and Alaska's Bristol Bay—has been afforded federal protection. Other special places could be added to this list without undermining the natural gas industry or increasing prices for consumers.

These protections are critical to saving our most sensitive marine ecosystems from the damaging consequences of drilling. Extracting oil or gas from beneath the ocean floor creates massive amounts of waste, including toxic metals and other contaminants, most of which is dumped untreated into surrounding waters. Offshore seismic exploration causes noise pollution harmful to whales and other marine mammals that depend on sound to communicate. Offshore development also brings with it the risk of toxic oil spills, which in turn threaten a wide variety of marine

*The sun sets over the Florida Keys. The Keys are one of the nation's few coastal treasures to receive federal protection from natural gas and oil drilling.*

species. And every well drilled generates tons of air pollutants. Congress should protect fragile areas of the U.S. Outer Continental Shelf, including waters off the East and West coasts, the eastern Gulf of Mexico, and offshore Alaska from the hazards of exploration and drilling.

## Maintain Existing Protections and Extend Protection to Other Special Places

Developing natural gas onshore can turn wildlands into industrialized zones. Well fields can cover thousands of acres and encompass hundreds, even thousands, of wells and drill pads. Each field is accompanied by a dense web of power lines, miles of pipelines and roads, waste pits, compressors, processing plants, and other production facilities. These activities degrade wildlife habitat, harm fragile soils, and encourage damaging off-road vehicle use.

Natural gas production on some public lands will continue to be necessary and should always be done in an environmentally responsible manner. But certain areas within the federal public lands system merit special protection from gas development. The energy production industry and its champions in Washington claim that these safeguards interrupt supply and cause price spikes. Yet according to a January 2003 report by the Interior, Energy, and Agriculture departments, only 12 percent of "technically recoverable" federal gas resources in the five major Western basins are totally off-limits to leasing and development—and most of that 12 percent is in lands that Congress has designated as wilderness and national parks.

*Natural gas fields dominate the scenery of a local bike path. Environmentalists oppose natural gas production that takes place near areas used for recreation.*

Protecting a few more remarkable pieces of America's natural heritage will not disrupt the industry. In fact, the industry is having trouble keeping up with the leases it already has: almost 73 percent of the total onshore acreage under oil and gas leases from the Bureau of Land Management is not in production. In the Rocky Mountains alone, only 32 percent of lands leased for gas drilling are in production. And more than half of the record number of drilling permits approved by the bureau in FY [Fiscal Year] 2004 went unused. Congress could designate more sensitive areas off-limits to drilling without harming the natural gas industry or consumers' pocketbooks. NRDC [Natural Resources Defense Council] recommends that Congress permanently protect several special places, including the Arctic National Wildlife Refuge, Utah's redrock canyon country, and Wyoming's Jack Morrow Hills in the heart of the Red Desert.

## Ensure That Pipelines Are Constructed in an Environmentally Sensitive Manner

Natural gas pipelines can significantly alter the landscape. To construct them, builders often carve networks of new roads through forests or coastal areas and dig miles and miles of trenches to lay the pipeline. Once in operation, pipelines have to be closely monitored to avoid dangerous leaks: pipelines are highly explosive and have been responsible for several deaths.

To minimize the impacts of natural gas pipelines, the federal government should issue rigorous siting and safety guidelines. Pipelines should not be routed through national parks, wildlife refuges, or wilderness areas. New pipelines should follow current rights-of-way whenever possible to take advantage of existing infrastructure and to avoid damaging sensitive wild places with pipeline construction or inadequate maintenance. For example, NRDC strongly opposes a pipeline that would carry Prudhoe Bay

*Environmentalists argue that natural gas pipelines should not be routed through national parks, wildlife refuges, or wilderness areas.*

gas that goes "over the top" offshore from the Arctic National Wildlife Refuge in Alaska to the MacKenzie Delta in the Northwest Territories in Canada. Instead, the natural gas pipeline should follow the existing Trans-Alaska Pipeline System and the Alaskan Highway. Finally, Congress should ensure that pipelines are safely maintained once they are in operation by providing adequate funding for inspection and enforcement.

## Plan an Alaska Gas Pipeline That Follows the Trans-Alaska Pipeline System and the Alaskan Highway

In Alaska's Prudhoe Bay region, geologic formations already drilled on state-owned lands contain at least 35 trillion feet of natural gas—equivalent to about one-fifth of all U.S proved reserves, or slightly less than two years' worth of nationwide

*A proposed natural gas pipeline would run next to the Trans-Alaska pipeline, the principal line that carries oil from Alaska to other destinations.*

consumption at current levels. A pipeline route linking these reserves to the U.S.-Canadian gas transmission system was approved almost 20 years ago, although it has not yet been constructed. According to the original plan, the pipeline would use existing rights-of-way and run parallel to Alaska's principal oil pipeline and the Alaskan Highway.

NRDC does not oppose construction of this system, as long as the earlier environmental reviews are updated according to U.S. and Canadian regulations and the project incorporates the best pipeline environmental and safety measures.

## Ensure Careful Siting and Environmental Guidelines for Liquefied Natural Gas

Liquefied natural gas (LNG) is natural gas that has been cooled to 261 degrees Fahrenheit below zero, reducing the volume of the gas 600-fold. Specially designed tankers can carry more than 2.5 billion cubic feet of gas per shipment, delivering LNG from around the globe to one of four U.S. marine terminals. Proposals have surfaced for at least 16 more import facilities to serve the U.S. market. But LNG facilities have very challenging siting requirements. LNG tankers are massive: they can only dock in harbors wide enough to allow the 900-foot-long tankers and deep enough to handle their 36-foot draft below the waterline. Extensive local opposition to LNG terminals and U.S. Coast Guard restrictions on LNG tanker movement further limit possible sites for new LNG facilities.

With careful siting, LNG can offer a valuable substitute for more environmentally destructive fuels. But increased use of LNG must not become a means for shifting natural gas exploration and extraction to especially sensitive areas, or to nations lacking adequate environmental and public-health safeguards. And all LNG siting decisions must analyze potential environmental and safety impacts and allow the public to participate in decision making. New facilities should also avoid marine sanctuaries, marine protected areas, and fragile resources like deep corals.

# America's Natural Gas Policies Will Not Prevent an Energy Crisis

## Julian Darley

According to Julian Darley in the following selection, America's energy policies do nothing to adequately address declining natural gas supplies. The U.S. energy plan provides for large tax breaks for the energy industry and opens up previously closed public lands for gas exploration. However, Darley contends that these measures are fruitless because America has few gas reserves left to tap. Moreover, the energy plan does not call on Americans to conserve energy, nor does it adequately fund the development of renewable energy sources. These measures—not increased drilling —would be the effective response to America's looming energy crisis. Darley is founder and director of the Post Carbon Institute, an organization helping communities with energy conservation and shrinking energy supplies.

Energy, despite being the core of existence and the real driver of the economy, is never a high policy priority for most governments, unless something dramatic happens to interrupt it or make it very expensive. In 2003, the United States became worried about high natural gas prices; then there was a string of huge electrical power blackouts across the industrialized world. Suddenly, for the first time in decades, energy was front-page news. With the impetus of some media attention, mainly negative, the U.S. government finally produced a much heralded and enormous new energy bill. It had been ten years since the last one, and this one had taken two years of secret deliberations and generated much acrimony from those kept out of the process, who happened to be the public. There was even a good deal of disagreement among those inside the process, namely Republicans and big corporations.

In the same year, after a rather more public process, Canada's National Energy Board also produced an energy plan, albeit in a slim volume. These plans, because of the way the United States dominates world energy markets and is deeply dependent on

*New York City is swathed in darkness following a major blackout in the summer of 2003. The blackout was one sign that an energy crisis could be on the horizon.*

Canadian energy reserves, are highly significant for the globe. They will affect the world for a long time to come. . . .

For those in the big energy industries, both the U.S. energy bill and the Canadian energy plan should come as a great relief or even a cause of joyful celebration. Both the U.S. bill and the Canadian plan show a fearless and reckless will to carry on with business as usual at all costs—though only if the costs are to be borne by the public.

## Canada Is Disconnected from Reality

The Canadian energy plan shows little understanding that the western Canadian Sedimentary Basin, which has supplied well over 80 percent of all Canada's gas, has peaked. Unlike the United States, there is little chance of Canada seeing the large coalbed methane and offshore supplement that has helped the United States delay dealing with its chronic overindulgence in gas. The Canadian plan consists of two separate scenarios—"techno-vert" and "supply push." The first suggests that some stress be laid on technological efforts to increase efficiency, so that more can be produced with less—a kind of BAU-lite (business-as-usual-lite). This scenario delivers about 3 percent annual growth and sees overall energy use increase by about 35 to 40 percent by 2025. The supply-push scenario, or undiluted BAU, makes no effort to conserve or be more efficient and thus predicts energy use to increase even more, though ironically this will deliver less growth than techno-vert. This is one reason why even some market fundamentalists and natural capitalists espouse green technology: it offers the chance of even more growth, not less. Both scenarios in the Canadian plan assume that domestic energy production will go on growing for the next few decades, much as it has done for the last two. It is a plan of almost surreal disconnection from reality, offering a choice between growth on stilts or growth on steroids.

## The U.S. Energy Bill

Though much longer and more detailed than the Canadian plan, the U.S. energy bill offers only one basic path, supply push as a ten-lane highway, though it does have scruffy little ditches on either side, called efficiency and renewables. In its own way it is equally surreal, though the authors, at least those in the White House, had been informed of the grim situations facing North American gas supply and world oil.

The bill offers about $20 billion worth of tax breaks, subsidies, and sundry giveaways, almost all of it to big U.S. energy industries and agricultural interests. The primary strategy is to open previously closed federal lands to exploration and extraction of natural gas and oil. The industry knows that gas is now the real prize, and for years the number of rigs looking for gas has outnumbered oil at around ten to one. The American public, however, is focused on oil, since that is already global, and very visibly causing a lot of trouble. The trouble may look new to some, but it is really as old as the oil business itself, and has become much more intense since the U.S. oil peak of 1970. In the United States, the petroleum industry more or less gave up

*Large reserves of oil and natural gas exist under the Gulf of Mexico, but some argue it is a mistake to continue to rely on fossil fuels.*

on oil twenty years ago but hasn't ever made a public announcement to that effect.

The second part of "letting the drill bit rip" is the streamlining of drilling-permit applications and easing of environmental restrictions on land. In the important gas-producing area of the Gulf of Mexico, royalty relief has been offered for companies undertaking deepwater exploration. All of this new streamlined drilling assumes that there is a lot of gas to find. At the natural gas crisis summit called by the U.S. Department of Energy in the summer of 2003, one of the most telling remarks was a plaintive call from an independent but long-established oil and gas producer. He ended his speech by calling on the government to allow his industry to go where they wanted, and he pledged that they would try to find the gas. The word "try" should have been pounced on by everyone in the room, but it was not. The industry knows that U.S. gas is going the same way as oil, but they would like a last bite of the taxpayers' wallet before they pack their bags and head for Russia, Africa, and, rather more reluctantly perhaps, the Arctic.

## Arctic Worries

The Arctic reluctance may stem less from fear of the cool temperatures in those parts than from industry worries that they cannot get enough money from the American taxpayer to subsidize the $20-billion pipeline needed to bring Alaskan gas to the Midwest, nor to guarantee a minimum price for the gas transported by that pipeline. Huge U.S. gas-price fluctuations have indeed played havoc with supply in the early years of the twenty-first century, but that is indicative of a declining system left prey to market forces. A minimum price guarantee is heresy to free-market purists, but without it, and enough federal involvement in the pipeline, North Slope Alaskan gas may never reach the lower forty-eight states. The Alaskan pipeline is being sold to labor interests as a huge job-creation package, with suggestions of up to 400,000 mostly unionized jobs being needed. This is a naked attempt to win Democratic support. Since the pipeline won't deliver gas to the United States before 2010, it certainly cannot be claimed that it will make the slightest difference to the gas gulf that has been opening up in North America since the turn of the century. . . .

## Ineffective Measures to Stave Off a Crisis

These are the more obvious measures designed to increase natural gas supply from underground. The draft energy bill contains many indirect measures, such as exemptions for water pollution and delaying the implementation of air quality laws, which will make CBM [coal bed methane] cheaper and easier to produce. Such measures will also reduce the amount of gas burned by power stations, not by reducing power demand or improving the efficiency of energy use, but by allowing more coal burning. There are tax breaks to encourage "clean coal technology," but even in the industry few think that it will make much difference before 2010. Hence the need to reduce air pollution controls. . . .

## Alternative Energy Schemes

In what might be called a parody of its own irrelevance, the U.S. energy bill is full of extraordinary subsidies for absurd schemes, the most remarkable being the ethanol section, which forces states to add increasing amounts of corn-produced ethanol to their gasoline to make it burn more cleanly. When you consider the net energy loss for the ethanol fuel it becomes ridiculous. In reality, the only thing this provision really helps are large, industrial agricultural corporations, which have given hundreds of thousands of dollars to the administration in campaign money and are now making millions back on the tax breaks. It is an example of the way energy pork is dressed up to look like energy policy. Another scheme that will do nothing to reduce natural gas use or increase energy independence is the effort to develop a hydrogen economy. While ethanol may be made from or with assistance from natural gas, at the moment hydrogen is almost exclusively made from natural gas. At least in the next few years, any large-scale attempts to switch to hydrogen cars will simply increase the pressure on already tight natural gas supplies. In fact, even industry proponents and the many environmentalists who have espoused hydrogen don't expect it to make much difference before 2010, by which time the United States may have a large and increasing LNG system in place. In other words, rather than importing foreign oil to run gas-guzzling cars, the United States, if world supplies allow, will be importing foreign LNG to run natural-gas guzzlers instead.

In the meantime, instead of trying to increase the fuel efficiency of the U.S. automobile system, which has seen no improvement since the early 1990s, the energy bill contains no fuel efficiency measures whatsoever, other than one paragraph proposing to investigate the possibility of reducing fuel use in cars starting in 2012. This is barely enough even for token or public-relations purposes, especially as the measure doesn't

"Winter Heating Costs to Soar. Where's the Supply? Is Somebody Wasting It?" Cartoon by Toles. *The Washington Post*, Sept. 26–October 2, 2005. Universal Press Syndicate. Reproduced by permission.

come with a single cent in appropriations. In other words, there is no money to pay for it. The current U.S. administration is either very confident or very certainly tempting providence.

Both as part of the need to increase electricity supply and as a possible way of producing hydrogen for the hydrogen economy as natural gas becomes too expensive or scarce, there are large provisions to increase nuclear power.

While the bill gives fortunes to nonsensical energy-losing schemes such as ethanol made from corn and the hydrogen economy, there are paltry sums for real renewables such as wind and solar, and just $6 million to encourage recycling. That's about 20¢ per head, hardly enough to buy one bicycle tire patch and some rubber cement.

## The Coming Energy Crisis

The U.S. draft energy bill represents a landmark of energy policy at its worst. It is almost impossible to see how it could be made any worse or more useless and inappropriate. The United States, and no doubt the world, will pay dearly for this bill, which is the quintessence of highly corrupt pork-barrel politics and payback for all the politicians that the oil and gas industry have bought. For average Americans, this bill is a surefire loser. If the oil and gas companies do find and deliver more supplies, it will only help prolong America's chronic and catastrophic hydrocarbon addiction by continuing the illusion of cheap and plentiful supply. Keeping prices down will make it still harder for renewable energy, largely unsupported by the corrupt subsidies so generously doled out to oil and gas, to make a serious contribution. If the oil and gas companies fail to find and deliver much new supply, especially of gas, then the United States will find itself in a full-blown energy crisis. If the U.S. luck with mild weather (just conceivably a by-product of the global warming it has likely helped to promote) carries on, and if the many LNG terminals are built, then the gas crisis will probably be put off past the 2004 election and then eased by large new influxes of LNG. This could just conceivably happen. If so, then America will carry on as normal for some further years, doing nearly nothing to reduce energy consumption or to develop a strong renewable energy infrastructure.

# Facts About Natural Gas

## The Composition of Natural Gas

Methane, 70–90 percent
Ethane, propane, butane, 0–20 percent
Carbon dioxide, 0–8 percent
Oxygen, less than 1 percent
Nitrogen, 0–5 percent
Hydrogen sulfide, 0–5 percent

Natural gas is made up of hydrocarbon gases. The major component of natural gas is methane. The methane molecule has one carbon atom and four hydrogen atoms, and it is represented by the symbol $CH_4$. When natural gas is used in the home, it is almost pure methane. In this state the gas is referred to as "dry." Before natural gas is refined and the other hydrocarbons are removed from the methane, the gas is referred to as "wet." In addition to the hydrocarbons listed above, natural gas can also include a trace of rare gases, including helium, neon, and xenon. Some of the hydrocarbons, including butane and propane, can be sold separately when removed from the natural gas.

## Composition of Liquefied Natural Gas

Methane, 95 percent
Other gases, 5 percent

Liquefied natural gas (LNG) is manufactured by refining natural gas and removing most of the associated hydrocarbon gases. Trace amounts of some gases may remain, including ethane, propane, butane, and nitrogen. The liquefied gas is then cooled to –260°F, reducing its volume to one six-hundredth that of regular natural gas. In January 2006, 39,466 million cubic feet of LNG was imported into the United States.

## Facts About Manufactured Gas

Manufactured gas, which consists mainly of carbon monoxide and hydrogen, was widely used in the nineteenth century, before the advent of electricity. Manufactured gas (also known as coal gas) was made by heating an organic material, mainly coal, to produce a flammable gas. This resulting gas could then be used for lighting and heating purposes. Portable manufactured gas lights made it possible to install lighting on railroad cars. In the early twentieth century, as natural gas became more prevalent, the use of manufactured gas greatly declined.

## Natural Gas Consumption

| | |
|---|---|
| Residential | 22 percent |
| Commercial | 13 percent |
| Industrial | 41 percent |
| Electric power generation | 18 percent |
| Transportation | 6 percent |

Natural gas provides more than 25 percent of U.S. energy needs. Residential consumption refers mainly to homes using natural gas for heating and air conditioning. Commercial consumption includes hospitals, office buildings, restaurants, and retail establishments that use natural gas for heating, cooking, air conditioning, and water heating. Industrial consumption includes factories and manufacturing facilities that use natural gas to make products and generate electricity. Electric power generation uses more and more natural gas; newer plants are built to be cleaner-burning than the predominant coal-burning plants, making them more popular. Transportation consumption includes vehicles that run solely on natural gas and vehicles that have been retrofitted to run on both natural gas and gasoline.

## Main Types of Natural Gas Drilling

Vertical drilling for natural gas involves drilling a borehole straight down to where the gas is expected to be. These types of wells can be dug quite deep. Horizontal drilling involves using a drilling assembly that is designed to drill at an angle instead of straight down. In horizontal drilling the bottom of the well can be anywhere from several hundred feet to more than ten thousand feet from the top borehole. Directional drilling involves drilling straight down from the initial borehole, angling the drilling assembly for a specific distance, and finishing by drilling straight down again. This type of drilling can allow several different areas to be drilled from the same drilling pad.

## Natural Gas Statistics for the United States

| | |
|---|---|
| Total 2005 gross withdrawals from gas wells | 17,302,168 million cubic feet |
| Total 2005 marketed natural gas production | 19,114,776 million cubic feet |
| Total 2005 natural gas pipeline imports | 3,654,089 million cubic feet |
| Total 2005 LNG imports | 631,258 million cubic feet |
| Total 2004 dry natural gas reserves | 192,513 billion cubic feet |
| Total 2004 number of producing gas wells | 405,048 |

These statistics show how much natural gas is actually produced and marketed in one year. In 2004 there were over four hundred thousand natural gas wells, each producing an average of 47.1 million cubic feet of marketed natural gas. The amount of natural gas consumed in the United States in 2005 was 21,980,633 million cubic feet. In addition, the United States exported 787,100 million cubic feet of natural gas. This figure includes 65,281 million cubic feet of LNG, mainly exported to Japan. These facts are available from the United States Energy Information Administration.

## U.S. Natural Gas Vehicle Statistics

| | |
|---|---|
| Number of natural gas vehicles | 130,000 |
| Number of natural gas fueling stations | 1,340 |
| Number of natural gas refueling appliances | 3,331 |

These statistics for natural gas vehicles include vehicles originally built to run on natural gas and vehicles that were originally built to run on gasoline and were later converted to run on natural gas. Many of the natural gas vehicles that are currently used in the United States are fleet vehicles. These vehicles are mainly used for public transportation and commerce. Although there are more than thirteen hundred natural gas refueling stations in the country, only about one-half are available for public use. Many of these refueling stations are for fleet vehicles only.

# Glossary

**appraisal wells:** Wells that are drilled to determine the size of a natural gas field.

**Arctic National Wildlife Refuge (ANWR):** A refuge located on the extreme northern border of Alaska along the Beaufort Sea and home to many species of wildlife and plants. Closed to energy development since its creation, the refuge is a major source of conflict in the search for natural gas. Many groups support drilling for natural gas in the refuge, and an equal number of groups say that the environmental impacts of natural gas drilling would destroy the refuge.

**bcf:** Billion cubic feet; a measurement for natural gas.

**biogas:** A gas by-product of decomposition of organic solids, usually in a landfill. The resulting gas consists of approximately 55 to 70 percent methane and 25 to 35 percent hydrogen, with trace amounts of other components (see **landfill gas**).

**Btu:** British thermal unit. One Btu is the amount of heat energy necessary to raise the temperature of one pound of water one degree Fahrenheit. Natural gas can be measured by how many Btu's are produced with the amount of gas used. The heat energy stored in one cubic foot of natural gas has over one thousand Btu's.

**coal bed methane:** Natural gas (methane) that is found trapped in the seams of coal beds. Coal can store up to six times the volume of natural gas as traditional gas beds. Hydraulic fracturing is necessary to extract natural gas from the coal beds.

**coal gas:** Another name for manufactured natural gas.

**coiled tubing:** Flexible, coiled drilling pipe used in place of regular rigid drilling pipe.

**compressed natural gas (CNG):** Natural gas that has been compressed into pressurized canisters for use and storage. Usually used for natural gas vehicles, the gas is normally compressed at either 3,000 or 3,600 psi (pounds per square inch).

**developmental wells:** The wells used to produce natural gas in a known gas field.

**directional drilling:** A type of drilling used to reach gas deposits that are in a different location than the drilling pad.

**discovery wells:** Exploratory wells that hit an area of natural gas.

**exploratory wells:** Wells that are drilled to locate natural gas. These wells are drilled in areas where natural gas has not previously been found.

**fossil fuels:** Fossil fuels were formed when ancient animals and plants died and were covered with sediment. The pressure of the sediment, combined with Earth's underground heat, transformed this organic material into fuel. Examples of fossil fuels are natural gas, coal, and petroleum (oil).

**fuel cell:** A device similar to a battery that uses a chemical process to change the energy content of fuel into electricity. Natural gas is largely used to generate the power in fuel cells.

**greenhouse gas:** An atmospheric gas that traps heat close to Earth. Burning fossil fuels releases carbon dioxide, which is considered a greenhouse gas.

**horizontal drilling:** A type of angled drilling used to reach gas deposits distant from the drilling pad. This type of drilling is often used to reach underwater gas deposits when the drilling pad is located onshore.

**hydraulic fracturing:** A drilling method for extracting natural gas from coal beds. A production well is drilled through rock to the coal seam containing the gas. Water is then pumped down the borehole to fracture the seam. The released gas follows the hydraulic fracture up the well to the surface.

**hydrogen-to-carbon ratio:** The amount of hydrogen and carbon that a fossil fuel produces. Natural gas has the highest hydrogen-to-carbon ratio of any hydrocarbon fossil fuel. This means that it has more hydrogen (what is wanted) and less carbon (what is not wanted).

**landfill gas:** Natural gas produced when organic material decomposes in a landfill. Also known as biogas (see **biogas**).

**liquefied natural gas:** Natural gas that has been cooled to −260°F. This cooling condenses the natural gas into a liquid form, which can be transported and stored in a much easier manner than can be the gaseous form of natural gas.

**manufactured natural gas:** Flammable gas that is produced by heating organic substances, usually coal. This type of gas was used for lighting purposes in the nineteenth century.

**methane:** A compound formed when animal and plant matter decays. This gas is the principal ingredient in natural gas. It is odorless, colorless, and tasteless.

**natural gas pipeline:** The conduit through which natural gas is transported. More than 1 million miles of natural gas pipeline exist in the United States. Gas is helped through the pipeline by a compressor. This machine increases the pressure of the gas, forcing it to move through the pipeline.

**natural gas reserves:** Known natural gas deposits that can be recovered with existing technology. When natural gas reserves are estimated, the total does not include natural gas reserves that cannot currently be recovered.

**natural gas resources:** All deposits of natural gas that are in the ground still waiting to be recovered.

**natural gas vehicles:** Vehicles that are designed to use natural gas as the primary source of fuel. Natural gas vehicles can reduce the exhaust emissions of carbon monoxide by up to 70 percent when compared to gasoline-powered vehicles. But studies have shown that natural gas–powered buses emit as many pollutants as diesel-powered buses.

**offshore drilling:** Drilling for natural gas in the oceans and gulfs many miles from the shoreline. Large drilling platforms are used to house the drilling apparatus needed to reach the gas. Offshore drilling can reach depths of more than ten thousand feet.

**reburning:** The process of injecting natural gas into oil- or coal-fueled boilers to decrease the amount of coal and oil needed for fuel.

**reservoir:** Huge underground storage facilities for natural gas. The storage areas are usually naturally occurring caves or human-made mines.

**sand fracturing:** The technique of using a mixture of liquid $CO_2$ and sand propants to enlarge existing cracks or create new cracks through which natural gas can flow out of the ground.

**seismic imaging:** The use of three- and four-dimensional computer models of subsurface layers of earth where natural gas is likely to be found. This allows drill teams to more accurately place drilling wells.

**slimhole drilling:** Using a smaller-than-normal drill bit to reach natural gas deposits. To be classified as slimhole, a drill bit must be less than six inches in diameter, as opposed to conventional drill bits, which can be up to twelve inches in diameter.

**tcf:** Trillion cubic feet; a measurement for natural gas.

# Chronology

**B.C.**
**1000**
Greeks find a flame caused by the spontaneous burning of natural gas on Mount Parnassus; a temple known as the Oracle of Delphi is constructed at the site.

**500**
Chinese begin using natural gas to desalinate and heat water.

**A.D.**
**ca. 1–99**
The king of Persia builds his palace kitchen around a natural gas flame.

**ca. 100–199**
Chinese begin searching for natural gas and make pipelines of bamboo.

**1620**
European settlers to the New World observe Native Americans igniting natural gas seeping from the Lake Erie area.

**1771**
George Washington acquires 250 acres in the West Virginia area because it contains a natural gas spring.

**1816**
Manufactured natural gas is used to illuminate the streets of Baltimore, Maryland; the gas is provided by what will become the Baltimore Gas & Electric Company.

**1821**
The first successful natural gas well is dug in Fredonia, New York; it is twenty-seven feet deep.

**1826**
In England, James Sharp invents the first natural gas cooker.

**1840**
The first industrial use of natural gas occurs; the gas is used to evaporate brine to make salt in Centerville, Pennsylvania.

**1858**
The first American natural gas company, Fredonia Gas Light Company in Fredonia, New York, is started.

**1859**
Colonel Edwin Drake digs a sixty-nine-foot-deep natural gas and oil well in Pennsylvania; a pipeline, two inches wide and five and a half miles long, is constructed to transport the natural gas to Titusville, Pennsylvania.

**1863**
Standardized natural gas metering begins, allowing gas companies to track exactly how much gas is being used by consumers; the American Meter Company in New York is the first company in the United States to provide metering.

**1880**
Natural gas–fueled stoves appear on the market in the United States.

**1885**
Robert Bunsen perfects the Bunsen burner, which mixes natural gas with air; Carl Auer von Welsbach develops the natural gas mantle, which is patented this year.

**1891**
The first lengthy natural gas pipeline is constructed in the United States; it transports gas 120 miles from natural gas wells in Indiana to Chicago.

**1904**
Natural gas is used to provide central heating and large-scale heating of water in London, England.

**1908**
The British thermal unit (Btu) is first used in Wisconsin.

**1915**
Large reservoirs of natural gas are discovered in Wyoming.

**1917**

The liquefaction method is successfully used to make liquefied natural gas (LNG); large-scale central heating fueled by natural gas is installed in a Baltimore, Maryland, housing development.

**1918**

Large natural gas deposits are discovered in the panhandle area of Texas.

**1922**

A large natural gas deposit is found in Kansas; this area, along with previous discoveries in Texas, becomes the Panhandle-Hugoton field, comprising at least 1.6 million acres.

**1925**

The first long-distance welded steel natural gas pipeline is laid between Louisiana and Beaumont, Texas; the pipeline is 217 miles long.

**1926**

Natural gas–fueled refrigerators are introduced in the United States.

**1931**

The first one-thousand-mile-long natural gas pipeline in the United States is built from Panhandle, Texas, to Chicago; the pipeline measures twenty-four inches in diameter.

**1937**

Natural gas–fueled air conditioning units are introduced in the United States; an undetected natural gas leak in New London, Texas, destroys Consolidated High School fifteen minutes before the end of the school day.

**1938**

The U.S. government begins regulating the natural gas industry.

**1943**

Natural gas is liquefied in Cleveland, Ohio.

**1951**

Natural gas is produced from underground coal in Spinney, England.

**1956**

Natural gas replaces heating oil as the principal fuel for central heating.

**1959**

Liquefied natural gas is produced for the first time on an industrial scale in Louisiana and shipped to Canvey Island, United Kingdom, on the first LNG tanker, a modified World War II freighter.

**1968**

For the first time in the United States the amount of natural gas consumed exceeds the amount of gas in reserve.

**1976**

Natural gas supply shortages occur during the winter of 1976–1977.

**1978**

Congress enacts the Natural Gas Policy Act of 1978, giving the Federal Energy Regulatory Commission (FERC) jurisdiction over intrastate and interstate natural gas production; Congress enacts the Powerplant and Industrial Fuel Use Act (FUA), banning the use of natural gas in new industrial boilers and electric power plants but not in existing facilities.

**1987**

President Ronald Reagan repeals any remaining restrictions imposed by the FUA and removes regulatory controls over natural gas resources.

**1996**

Natural gas customers are able to purchase gas from companies other than their local natural gas supplier.

**2005**

The Bureau of Land Management decides not to open the Rocky Mountain Front to natural gas development.

# For Further Reading

## Books

Rebecca L. Busby, ed., *Natural Gas in Nontechnical Language*. Tulsa, OK: PennWell, 1999.

Julian Darley, *High Noon for Natural Gas: The New Energy Crisis*. White River Junction, VT: Chelsea Green, 2004.

Richard Heinberg, *The Party's Over: Oil, War, and the Fate of Industrial Societies*. Gabriola Island, BC: New Society, 2003.

Thomas O. Miesner and William L. Leffler, *Oil and Gas Pipelines in Nontechnical Language*. Tulsa, OK: PennWell, 2006.

F. William Payne, ed., *User's Guide to Natural Gas Technologies*. Lilburn, GA: Fairmont, 1999.

## Periodicals

Miguel Bustillo, "It's Not All Blue Skies for Drilling Project," *Los Angeles Times*, January 29, 2005.

Rodger Dayle, "By the Numbers: Energy Geopolitics," *Scientific American*, October 2004.

William L. Fisher, "Natural Gas: The Coming Methane Economy," *Geotimes*, November 2002.

David Hogberg and James Dellinger, "Here's the Drill," *American Spectator*, December 8, 2005.

Tom Knudson, "New Alarm Sounded for Canada's Forest," *Sacramento Bee*, May 4, 2003.

Raymond J. Kopp, "Natural Gas: Supply Problems Are Key," *Resources*, Winter 2005.

Barbara Maynard, "Fire in Ice," *Popular Mechanics*, April 2006.

John G. Mitchell, "Tapping the Rockies," *National Geographic*, July 2005.

Lisa M. Pinsker, "Coalbed Methane: The Future of U.S. Natural Gas?" *Geotimes*, November 2002.

Charles Pope, "Alaska Wildlife Refuge's Fate Again Hangs in Balance," *Seattle Post-Intelligencer*, February 28, 2005.

John Riordan, "Meeting Natural Gas Demand: Infrastructure Is Important, Technology Is Key," FAS *Public Interest Report*, Autumn 2003.

Robert F. Service, "The Carbon Conundrum," *Science*, August 13, 2004.

Megan Sever, "Alaska's New Pipeline," *Geotimes*, December 2004.

## Internet Sources

Alternative Energy Institute, "Natural Gas: Enticing, Yes, but a Panacea?" www.altenergy.org.

Michael Barratt, "Point: Safe Oil Drilling in Lakes Is Possible," September 10, 2001. www.glrc.org.

The Center for Liquefied Natural Gas, "Liquefied Natural Gas and America's Future." www.lngfacts.org.

CH-IV International, "LNG Fact Sheet." www.ch-iv.com.

Paul K. Driessen, "It's Time to Support ANWR Drilling," December 19, 2005. www.enterstageright.com.

Federal Regulatory Energy Commission, "A Guide to LNG: What All Citizens Should Know." www.ferc.gov/industries/lng.asp.

International Association for Natural Gas Vehicles, "SwRI Compares Emissions from Low-Emission Diesel and Natural Gas School Buses," November 20, 2002. www.iangv.org.

Praful Mangalath, "What Is Natural Gas and History of Use," 2003. www.las.colorado.edu.

Kim McGuire, "EPA Backs Effort to Cut Drilling Haze," October 12, 2005. www.denverpostbloghouse.com/washington.

Natural Gas Supply Association, "Natural Gas and Technology," 2004. www.naturalgas.org.

Natural Gas Vehicle Coalition, "Natural Gas Vehicles: The Environmental Solution Now," May 2003. www.ngvc.org.

Natural Resources Defense Council, "Creating a Responsible Natural Gas Policy," April 2005. www.nrdc.org.

Public Interest Research Group in Michigan, "Dirty Drilling: The Threat of Oil and Gas Drilling in Michigan's Great Lakes," 2003. www.pirgm.org.

Sierra Club, "Energy Efficiency: Cleaner, Faster, Cheaper." www.sierraclub.org.

## Web Sites

**Natural Gas Supply Association** (www.naturalgas.org). This association of natural gas producers and marketers promotes the use of natural gas as an excellent source of environmentally friendly energy. The NGSA Web site includes information on all aspects of natural gas, including use, history, exploration, production, distribution, market activity, regulation, the environment, and technology.

**Natural Gas Vehicle Forum** (www.ngv.org). The Natural Gas Vehicle Forum Web site offers information on many aspects of natural gas vehicles, including vehicle benefits, safety information, and engine overviews. The Web site has links to filling station information and specific vehicle listings. The site also includes information on funding for purchasing a natural gas vehicle.

**Natural Resources Defense Council** (www.nrdc.org). This environmental organization provides information concerning the effects of natural gas on the environment. Their Web site also provides information on cleaner uses of natural gas and ways to reduce and conserve the amount of natural gas that is used.

**U.S. Department of Energy** (www.doe.gov). The Department of Energy Web site provides information on natural gas statistics in the United States. The Energy Information Adminstration provides natural gas statistics, including production and consumption for industry and home consumption, storage information, pricing, and delivery information. The Office of Natural Gas Regulatory Activities provides information on natural gas imports and exports. Links to alternative uses and sources for natural gas are also provided.

# Index

# Picture Credits

Cover: © Royalty-Free/CORBIS
© Andre Jenny/Alamy, 44
Andrew Sacks/Getty Images, 12
AP/ Wide World Photos, 15, 30, 37, 47, 67, 68, 78, 82, 83, 84, 89
© G. P. Bowater/Alamy, 40, 60
Jacques Descloitres, MODIS Rapid Response Team, NASA/GSFC, 42
Jean-Pierre Pieuchot/Getty Images, 11
John Dominis/Time Life Pictures/Getty Images, 17
Johnny Johnson/Getty Images, 56
Kristin Finnegan/Getty Images, 97
© Layne Kennedy/CORBIS, 51
© Lester Lefkowitz/CORBIS, 75
© Mike Zens/CORBIS, 25
Photos.com, 55 (inset), 61, 71, 88
Robert Everts/Getty Images, 29
Robert Nickelsberg/Liaison/Getty Images, 91
Reuters/Landov, 38
Spencer Platt/Getty Images, 95
Steve Zmina, 20, 23, 27, 31, 33, 35, 45, 50, 54, 62, 77
Steven J. Kazlowski/Alamy, 55 (main)
Tony Waltham/Robert Harding World Imagery/Getty Images, 92
Tyler Stableford/Getty Images, 64

# About the Editor

Carrie Fredericks received her BA from Detroit's Wayne State University, majoring in English and minoring in general science studies. She has worked on Thomson/Gale publications for 15 years. This is her first publication for Greenhaven Press. She resides, with her family, in Michigan.